LONDON'S ROYAL PARKS

Paul Rabbetts

SHIRE PUBLICATIONS

Published in Great Britain in 2014 by Shire Publications
Ltd, PO Box 883, Oxford, OX1 9PL, UK.

PO Box 3985, New York, NY 10185-3985, USA.

E-mail: shire@shirebooks.co.uk   www.shirebooks.co.uk

© 2014 Paul Rabbitts.

A CIP catalogue record for this book is available from the
British Library.

Shire Library no. 793.   ISBN-13: 978 0 74781 370 5

Paul Rabbitts has asserted his right under the Copyright,
Designs and Patents Act, 1988, to be identified as the
author of this book.

Designed by Tony Truscott Designs, Sussex, UK
and typeset in Perpetua and Gill Sans.

Printed in China through Worldprint Ltd.

14 15 16 17 18   10 9 8 7 6 5 4 3 2 1

COVER IMAGE
The beautiful vista from Greenwich Park, looking across
the Queen's House and Royal Naval College, and over
the Thames to the Docklands. Photograph courtesy of
Kit Moc.

TITLE PAGE IMAGE
A view through the Canada Gate (1905) at Green Park.

DEDICATION
Dedicated to my beautiful daughter Holly Rabbitts.

ACKNOWLEDGEMENTS
I would like to thank the following for assisting me in
producing this book on London's Royal Parks, the greatest
network of parks in any city in the world: Dr Stewart
Harding and David Lambert of the Parks Agency for
lending me countless images over the years and for being
proper 'Parkies'; the following from the Royal Parks,
Douglas Rowland at Bushy Park; Nick Biddle at Regent's
Park; Simon Richards at Richmond Park; Richard Flenley
from Land Use Consultants; Philip Norman from the
Garden Museum; Russell Butcher from Shire Publications;
Deborah Brady from Watford Borough Council for those
fantastic photographs; Jimmy Page and Robert Plant for
inspiration, and my lovely family for accompanying me on
the many jaunts into these and many other parks,
yesterday, today and tomorrow.

I would also like to thank the people who have allowed me
to use illustrations, which are acknowledged as follows:

Alamy, pages 28 and 30, The Royal Parks, pages 62, 63, 65
(bottom), 66, 68, 70, 85 (top and bottom); Louise Allen,
page 22; The Bridgeman Art Library, pages 8, 10 (top), 12,
14 (bottom), 16–17, 32, 37 (bottom left), 80, 86 (top),
91; The British Library, pages 13, 24–5, 26, 35, 36, 54
(bottom), 74–5 (bottom); Museum of London, page 10
(bottom); Deborah Brady, title page, pages 19 (bottom),
20, 28, 29 (both), 40; Fox Photos/Getty Images, page 18;
Jesus College, Oxford, page 64; Lamport Hall Collection,
page 90; The Parks Agency, page 71 (bottom); Illustrated
London News, pages 42 (top and bottom), 43; Fitzwilliam
Museum, page 88; © TfL from the London Transport
Museum, page 100. All other photographs and images are
from the author's collection.

Shire Publications is supporting the Woodland Trust, the UK's leading woodland conservation charity, by funding the dedication of trees.

CONTENTS

INTRODUCTION

THE Honourable Mrs Evelyn Cecil wrote in 1907: 'London has a peculiar fascination of its own and to a vast number of English-speaking people all over the world, it appeals with irresistible force.' So much has been said and written about it that the theme might seem to be worn out, yet there are still fresh aspects to present, still hidden charms to discover and re-discover, and still deep problems to solve. London is also the classic example of the scattered city, as against the concentrated city such as Paris, and many observers still often analyse London as a network of villages. As Cecil writes:

> The huge unwieldy mass, which cannot be managed or legislated for as other towns, but has to be treated as a county, enfolds within its area all the phases of human life. It embraces every gradation from wealth to poverty, from the millionaire to the pauper alien. The collection of buildings which together make London are a most singular assortment of innumerable variations between beauty and ugliness, between palaces and works of art and hovels of sordid and unlovely squalor.

Thankfully, much has changed since 1907. Cecil continues:

> ... the parks and gardens of London form bright spots in the landscape ... they are beyond the pale of controversy; they appeal to all sections of the community, to the workers as well as the idlers, to the rich as well as to the poor, to the thoughtful as well as the careless. From the utilitarian point of view they are essential ... the part they play in brightening the lives of countless thousands cannot be overestimated.

The various parks and gardens at the turn of the twentieth century were grouped into three classes: the Royal Parks; those maintained by the London County Council; and those coming under the many Borough Councils.

Many people still believe that London owes its unique charm not so much to its historical associations, or its extraordinary variety of buildings, as to

its parks — and in particular, the Royal Parks. For several centuries, the reigning sovereigns of Britain have allowed members of the general public to enter their parks and to enjoy themselves there; on certain occasions, when some of their less benevolent or more officious subjects have wished to take this privilege away, they have taken steps to see that it should be preserved. This has not always been the case, however. It may have been an urge for greater privacy, for instance, that led Queen Caroline, wife of King George II, to ask the Prime Minister, Sir Robert Walpole, what it would cost to restrict the use of St James's Park to members of the Royal Family. Walpole's famous sonorous reply – 'Only three Crowns, Madam' – was sufficiently intimidating to deter the Queen from her purpose.

As the population of London increased during the eighteenth and nineteenth centuries, it became more and more difficult for the officials of the Crown to preserve the amenities of the Royal Parks in and near the capital, and to control the behaviour of those admitted to them. From 1851, the duties were transferred by the Crown, through Parliament, to the Office of Works and Public Buildings. The 1851 Act originally vested those powers in the Commissioners of Works but the powers were transferred to the Minister of Works in 1942. Following a number of transfers, the powers now rest with the Secretary of State for Culture, Media and Sport. As Hunter Davies wrote in 1983 in *A Walk Round London's Parks*, the Royal Parks are London's greatest glory and offer so much, from playgrounds to palaces, Wren to Rembrandt, mausoleums to mosques, ponds to polo. London's Royal Parks taken as a whole are unrivalled. Their variety and irregularity are their charm, and no description of them can be given as a whole. Each has its own associations and its own unique history dating back centuries and a historical legacy overall aligned with nothing less than the history of England.

Blackman Street, London, by John Atkinson Grimshaw (1836–93).

ST JAMES'S PARK: A PARK OF GREAT MAJESTY

ST JAMES'S PARK is in many ways the most romantic and beautiful of the Royal Parks and symbolises much of the English tradition; its visitors experience the majesty of the historic buildings surrounding it and take great pleasure in strolling among its avenues of trees, lawns and formal flower beds. The adjacent palaces and royal residences such as Buckingham Palace, Clarence House, Marlborough House and, of course, St James's Palace, all add to the majesty of this, the most supremely royal of all the parks. To the south stretches Whitehall, the site of one of the most romantic palaces of all, and parts of its other sides are bounded by a long terrace that commemorates Carlton House, the Prince Regent's palatial London residence, and by the barracks of the Brigade of Guards, the reigning sovereign's personal bodyguard.

However, its origins date from 1533 when Henry VIII married Anne Boleyn and immediately took an interest in a nearby hospital that stood in the midst of fields. The hospital had been dedicated to a St James, possibly the first Bishop of Jerusalem, and was located not far from Charing Cross. At the time, it was a hospital for female patients only who were allegedly suffering from the foul disease of leprosy. Henry's interest was based solely on his desire for a private country home, not too far from the palace of Whitehall, where he could continue to hold his courts. Without hesitation, he threw out the occupants, had the building pulled down and erected 'a goodly manor'. King Henry lost no time in surrounding himself with all the contemporary aids to his amusement. Having spent most of his early life at Greenwich, which had a well-stocked deer park, Henry had to have one for his new home and therefore took in the marshy fields that surrounded the old hospital and enclosed them as the private demesne of his new palace, and set up in them a nursery for deer. Beyond the palace and its gardens, the entire estate was surrounded by a fine brick wall, making St James's the first of the Royal Parks to be enclosed. It was here that Henry VIII created a suitable place for royal enjoyment and for military reviews, with a tilt-yard, his deer park, and a tennis court and bowling green. At its northeast corner there

Opposite: Looking towards the London Eye from St James's Park.

7

St James's Park was a popular place for promenading. Colourfully dressed figures are shown walking along the Mall with St James's Palace on the left and Westminster Abbey in the distance on the right. Stags and fallow deer graze on the right in the Park. The formal layout is shown by the regimented planting of trees, receding into the distance.

was a rural garden for relaxation and refreshment with a yard, a pond for bathing and some butts where shooting could be practised – at the time called the 'Spring Garden'. Anne Boleyn, however, did not have long to enjoy the pleasures of St James's. Within three years she was imprisoned in the Tower and ultimately beheaded.

On the death of Elizabeth in 1603, James VI of Scotland succeeded to the English throne as James I of England. He left his mark on St James's Park acquiring a menagerie of exotic animals, such as crocodiles, which he kept in the ponds not far from the palace; hawks and pelicans, from the Grand Duke of Muscovy; antelopes, from the Great Mogul; a leopard, from the King of Savoy's collection; and the most notable attraction, an elephant acquired in Spain by George Villiers, Duke of Buckingham.

Henry, Prince of Wales, the eldest son of James, enjoyed many manly pursuits, including hunting deer, but preferred the chase to the kill. However, with his tragic death at the age of eighteen in 1612, it was his younger brother who succeeded to the throne, as Charles I. His impact on the park was minimal but on the morning of his execution Charles I took his last walk across St James's Park, dressed in a black cloak, preceded and followed by detachments of soldiers with banners flying and drums rolling. At the corner

of the park nearest to the Spring Garden, he apparently turned to take a last look at a tree that had been planted here, in much happier times, by his brother Prince Henry.

It was Charles II who, on his return from exile abroad, re-created St James's Park to look rather more as we know it today. Whilst in exile in France, he had been greatly influenced by the grandeur of such landscapes the grounds of Versailles. On his return to England, he would have noticed the badly drained ground to the south of St James's Palace, and seen that most of the previous landscape had been destroyed, the trees having been cut down to provide fuel for impoverished citizens. He ordered at once that the rough ground separating his principal London homes should be laid out with pleasant walks and flower beds, like the palaces he had seen in France. He took advice from the great French garden architect André le Nôtre, was 'of the opinion that the natural simplicity of this Park, its rural and in some places wild character, had something more grand than he could impart to it', and persuaded the King not to change it to the extent he wished. Charles II pressed on in more modest fashion and French landscaper André Mollet was probably ultimately responsible for the laying out of the park. The first step was the digging of a canal 2,800 feet long and 120 feet wide, which ran straight across the length of the park from the Whitehall end to the edge of the Mulberry Garden. Such a canal was the central feature of the French gardens. With Horse Guards as the point of departure, avenues would radiate on each side of the canal in what is known as the *patte d'oie* ('goose-foot') pattern. The design of St James's Park never achieved the geometrical perfection of other André le Nôtre gardens: it was a relatively undisciplined pattern with the Mall on the right and Birdcage Walk on the left. The canal and avenues were lined with double rows of saplings, but then the development in French style seems to have petered out. One pond was left in Charles's revamped park: Rosamond's Pond was allowed to remain more or less as it had been and during the times of the Stuart kings became a favourite meeting place for society ladies 'on the loose' and their clandestine lovers; later it was given the name of 'Suicide Pond' because of the desperate maidens who, disappointed in love, or by lovers who never turned up, plunged into it and drowned themselves.

Charles II, like his father, was fond of exotic animals and birds, and this is commemorated by the name given to the road that runs along the south margin of the park – 'Birdcage Walk' – for it was here that the king had a long range of aviaries set up. 'Storey's Gate' was named after Edward Storey, Keeper of the King's Birds, whose house is believed to have stood at this spot. The most curious of the birds were the two pelicans given to Charles by the Russian ambassador, living among a range of other waterfowl on a small island at the western end, which came to be known as Duck Island. Charles had also become

St James's Park and the Mall, after 1745 (oil on canvas), attributed to Joseph Nickolls (fl. 1713–55).

Coloured engraving of St James's Park, The Mall, c. 1750, by Robert Sayer.

an enthusiastic player of *paille maille* in France, where it was fashionable at court. This was a game that had originated in Italy in the Middle Ages (and was described as a strenuous kind of croquet), so obviously St James's Park had to have a royal *paille maille* alley. The site chosen for the new royal alley was just inside the northern wall of the park. On the other side of the wall ran an ancient highway, running past St James's Palace heading west. Charles was a reasonably

good player but became agitated because of the clouds of dust that were stirred up by carriages on the old highway just over the park wall. In 1661 Charles decided enough was enough, fenced off the old highway, and created a new road along the tree-lined avenue that ran parallel to it. It was originally called Catherine Street, but most Londoners were not impressed with the name and it became known locally as Pall Mall.

The park flourished, and the monarch was often to be seen strolling among those subjects who were allowed access to promenade, frequently doing so unattended. In hard winters, the canal in the park was a popular choice with skaters. The building of houses along Pall Mall was slow at first, except for St James's Palace and a small group of buildings at the eastern end. It was Charles's enterprising friend Henry Jermyn who started to develop the fields to the north of Pall Mall with houses for aristocrats and the very rich (including the king's mistress, Nell Gwyn), so they could enjoy from there an uninterrupted view across St James's Park.

In spite of the strictness of the regulations concerning quarrelling and duelling in St James's Park, standards of behaviour deteriorated, especially during the eighteenth century, until the place became notorious for scandal. It became a noted haunt of whores of both sexes. By the 1760s, the state of the park was so notorious that protests in the local newspapers were commonplace, primarily covering violence in the park itself. Although it was locked at night, thousands of people had unofficial keys and the park was frequented at night by off-duty soldiers. It was demanded that Rosamond's Pond be filled in, and stagnant channels surrounded the duck decoy at the western end of the canal. These were described as:

St James's Park
(oil on canvas),
George Morland
(1763–1804).

> ... so noxious to the health of the neighbouring inhabitations, especially in Downing Street and Duke Street, from the aquatic and stinking exhalations of those waters ... which disagreeably and even dangerously affect all persons who walk or inhabit thereabouts ...

Reforms were under way by 1766 but with little impact. By 1770 the landscape was partly remodelled by 'Capability' Brown, with Rosamond's Pond filled in – this seemed to encourage the Bow Street Justices to further their intentions in issuing warrants to arrest the disorderly 'till St James's Park and its environs be brought into that state of decorum that his

Majesty's subjects may enjoy the privilege of walking and passing through that delightful spot without nuisance or interruption'. The Gordon Riots of 1780 were an anti-Catholic protest against the Papists Act 1778 and caused significant panic in London; as a result several regiments of militia moved in and set up camp in St James's Park, with long lines of tents extending from east to west, visited daily by George III.

St James's Palace had become the principal home of the Royal Family after the palace of Whitehall was destroyed in 1698 by a fire. But by 1762, George III had become disenchanted with St James's Palace and had now purchased the town residence of the Dukes of Buckingham – a house surrounded by fields. St James's Palace became used just for court ceremonies and as a home for junior members of the Royal Family.

Despite the apparent falling out of favour of St James's Palace and the king's relocation to Buckingham House, St James's Park continued to be important to the Royal Family, primarily because it has always been on the doorstep of their principal London home. As a result it has been the scene of celebrations, processions and mourning. At the defeat of Napoleon, the Prince Regent invited the heads of all the friendly countries to London, and was determined to entertain them with no expense spared. Over the canal in St James's Park, within easy walking distance of Buckingham House, the Prince had a great Chinese-style bridge put up, designed by his favourite architect, John Nash, and on this bridge the Prince had a great seven-storeyed

*View of
St James's Park with
Westminster Abbey
Beyond (oil on
canvas) by
John Inigo Richards
(1731–1810).*

pagoda built, similar in design to the one erected in the gardens at Kew. This was to be illuminated with gas lights and 'brilliant fireworks … to be displayed from every division of the lofty Chinese structure'. The Pagoda was stunning and an incredible spectacle, but structurally unsafe. While the assembled 'Top People of Victorious Europe' were still congratulating their enterprising host, his Chinese Pagoda began to sway and within minutes started to belch out smoke, burst into flames and fell with a deafening crash into the canal, which was still surrounded by admiring crowds. Two spectators were killed and many were injured.

The Chinese Bridge and Pagoda, erected in the Park to commemorate the Glorious Peace of 1814.

From the middle of the eighteenth century, the fashion for landscape gardening was at its height. 'Capability' Brown had done his work of destruction, and set the fashion for 'copying nature', and his successors were following along the same lines, but going much further even than Brown. The sight of a straight canal had become intolerable. The Serpentine was designed when the idea was dawning that it might be possible to make the banks of artificial sheets of water in anything but a perfectly straight line was just dawning, and the canal in St James's Park was transformed when half the stiff ponds and canals in the kingdom had been twisted and turned into lakes or meres.

A map of
St James's Park
drawn by Knyff
(c. 1662), showing
the Grand Canal
lined with trees,
as laid out by
André Mollet.

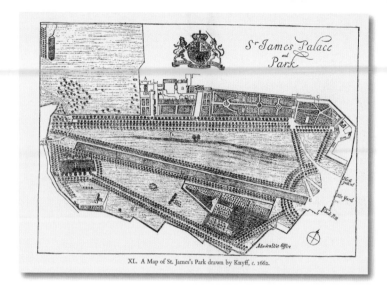

XL. A Map of St. James's Park drawn by Knyff, c. 1662.

Brown had had a hand in the alterations at the time Rosamond's Pond was removed, but it was Nash who planned and executed the work fifty years later. It was begun in 1827, and a contemporary writer praises the result as 'the best obliteration of avenues' that had been effected. Although he accepts it involved 'a tremendous destruction of fine elms', he is lost in admiration of the 'astounding ingenuity' which 'converted a Dutch canal into a fine flowing river, with incurvated banks, terminated at one end by a planted island and at the other by a peninsula'.

Plan of the
proposed
alterations to
St James's Park.
Coloured
engraving,
English school,
nineteenth century.

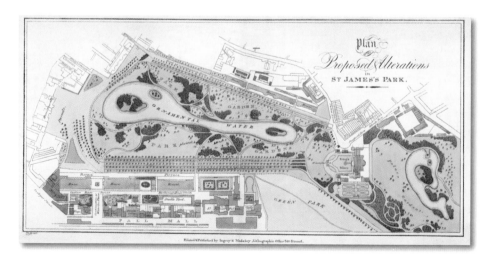

Just before the alterations began, and the complete transformation of the canal was taken in hand, the park was lit with gas lamps, an innovation which caused much excitement. At the same time orders were issued to shut the gates by ten o'clock every evening. Nash's framework for the new St James's Park was the Mall on the north side, Birdcage Walk on the south, Horse Guards Parade on the east and the new Buckingham Palace rising on the west. He built terraces on the site and grounds of Carlton House, since given up by the Prince Regent. His proposal for a number of lodges was never executed, and the Mall, which he proposed to form into a quadruple avenue for carriages, riders and pedestrians, was considerably modified in execution.

Another addition was the 120-foot-tall Aberdeen granite column that was erected in memory of the late Duke of York, son of King George III. The cost of the column, with statue by Sir Richard Westmacott, was £26,000, which was raised by public subscription, and created much ill feeling. Further works included the removal of the 1814 bridge and handsome iron railings were erected around the park; the Birdcage Walk was also levelled. By the 1830s, Nash's grand project had been largely completed. The Prince, who had become George IV, died in 1830, without seeing the completion of Buckingham Palace, and was succeeded by his brother, the Duke of Clarence, as William IV. Throughout the nineteenth century, Government officials continually sought to convert St James's Park from a private royal preserve into an accessible public amenity. By 1856, some greater public access had been agreed to the wider masses, and requests for covered seating were

The monument to Prince Frederick, Duke of York, the commander-in-chief of the British Army during the French Revolutionary Wars. The great height of the column – 123 feet 6 inches (37.64 metres) – caused wits to suggest that the Duke was trying to escape his creditors, as he died £2 million in debt.

Buckingham Palace: from St James's Park, 1842, by Thomas Shotter Boys (1803–74).

received in 1860 along with requests for boating on the lake. The Ornithological Society had also been given permission to build a cottage on Duck Island and later an aviary and two boathouses were added.

The park did, however, suffer a significant loss of land and amenity when the vast Queen Victoria Memorial, on its island site, and the surrounding crescent-shaped gardens, were constructed in front of Buckingham Palace

in 1911. The lake was shortened and over a hundred trees were felled. The Mall by this time, as Nash had hoped, had become a triumphal way when the Admiralty Arch was built in 1910, linking Trafalgar Square and beyond to the Mall and the St James's Park complex. With the advent of the First World War, there were significant changes to the park, echoing the deprivations of the period. Its lake was drained and staff from the

Members of the public, some waving the cardboard cases carrying their gas masks, file down into a shelter in St James's Park, on 3 September 1939 during the first air raid alert, on the day Britain declared war against Germany.

nearby government departments overflowed into temporary offices set up along its dry bed. With the start of the Second World War, despite being targeted by the Luftwaffe, Buckingham Palace and St James's Park remained unaffected although a number of bomb shelters were constructed in the park.

The remaining monuments and statuary in St James's Park are to be found mainly around its perimeter, with the inner park containing only a few small buildings and Eric Bedford's bridge, which was built in 1957 in place of the original suspension bridge dating from 1857. Bedford also designed the iconic Cake House, opened in 1970 by Mrs Harold Wilson; this was replaced in 2005 by Inn The Park, a new refreshment facility for the park's five million visitors a year. Not far from the Inn is the impressive Guards Memorial, erected in 1922 and designed by H. Carlton Bradshaw with sculpture by Gilbert Ledward. The five soldiers aligned in front of the cenotaph represent the Grenadier, Coldstream, Scots, Irish and Welsh Guards. Ledward is one of the few artists to have devoted himself entirely to war memorials. But it is the Queen Victoria Memorial at the end of Aston Webb's processional route from Admiralty Arch to a grand *rond-point* in front of Buckingham Palace that most visitors to London and St James's Park remember. Completed in 1911, it lay south of the original Pall Mall and forms a perfect foil to both St James's Park and the adjacent Green Park.

St James's Park, now fully restored, is one of the most popular of the Royal Parks in London. The walk around it is now understandably one of the most fashionable promenades in London, where well-known politicians can often be seen alongside office workers. It is still a magnet for the many visitors from around the world who continue to enjoy London's rich pageantry on such occasions as royal weddings, coronations, state funerals and other national celebrations, including the Golden and Diamond jubilees of Queen Elizabeth II.

The palace of Whitehall was destroyed by fire in 1698 and much of the site was then built over. Today the view from St James's Park towards the government offices of Whitehall beyond Horse Guards Parade is one of London's most familiar sights.

Buckingham Palace from St James's Park in 1905.

Buckingham Palace today: the area outside the palace was remodelled between 1906 and 1924 to make space for the Queen Victoria Memorial. Osbert Sitwell described it, viciously, as 'tons of allegorical females in white wedding cake marble, with whole litters of their cretinous children'.

GREEN PARK: A PARK OF SIMPLE BEAUTY

A T FIFTY-ONE ACRES, and set in a magnificent site between Piccadilly and Constitution Hill, with Buckingham Palace and the Victoria Memorial Gardens beyond, and at its eastern boundary the Queen's Walk, running down from the Ritz Hotel to Lancaster House in the Mall, Green Park would appear to have a lot to enthuse about. But, in reality, not much has happened there for many years. Green Park has had its great days, when the paths were frequented by the fashionable and beautiful; it was also the scene of two spectacular disasters, and assassins have lurked among the trees waiting to shoot at royalty driving to or from the palace.

When Charles II returned from Europe and reclaimed his throne, the land between the wall of St James's Palace and what ultimately became known as Piccadilly was waste ground and meadow. Two low hills were planted with a few willow trees, and the ground was crossed by a variety of ditches. It was Charles who enclosed at least 36 acres with a high brick wall; the land within became known as the Upper St James's Park, and here he set up a deer harbour. Another 41 acres were added to the west. Avenues of trees were planted, formal gravelled paths were laid down and a Ranger's Lodge was built for the official in charge. In the centre of his new park, Charles II built a 'snow house and an ice-house, as the mode is in some parts of France and Italy, and other hot countries, for to cool wines and other drinks for the summer season'.

Many new houses were also built on St James's Fields, which flanked the park on the east, and along Piccadilly, to the north, several grand mansions appeared. There were, however, significant differences between the Upper St James's Park and Lower St James's Park. In the Upper Park there were no restrictions on 'sword-drawing', so it became a favourite resort for duels. In January 1696 Sir Henry Colt, who had been challenged by 'Beau' Fielding, fought a duel with his adversary here in the late evening, probably in full view of his mistress, the Duchess of Cleveland. Fielding is said to have run his opponent through his body before the baronet could even draw his sword, but in spite of this serious wound Sir Henry managed to disarm Fielding

Opposite:
Canada Gate:
Victorian detail at
its most glorious.

21

The Bason in the Green Park, St James's. Coloured engraving, showing a general view of the park with buildings in the background. First published in Ackermann's *Repository of Arts*, Plate 22, Volume 4.

and ended the fight, with both men surviving the bloody duel. Many more such incidents followed.

The eighteenth century saw many further improvements to Upper St James's Park. At the northeast end a canal or reservoir was excavated, which was enlarged in 1730 to enable the Chelsea Water Company to provide for the growing needs of St James's Palace, the park and Buckingham House. The reservoir was embellished with a lively but decorative fountain, which became known as 'The Queen's Basin' at around the same time as 'The Queen's Walk' was being laid out along the eastern boundary. Queen Caroline, wife of George II, who had been making many improvements around the Palace at Kensington, took great interest in Upper St James's Park and gave orders for the laying out of a private walk so that members of the Royal Family might divert themselves there in the spring, without being too much disturbed by the general public. At the Mall end she had built, to designs by William Kent, 'The Queen's Library' – in reality this was nothing more than a summerhouse overlooking the park. Several accounts relate that she caught a cold walking there before breakfast on 9 November 1737 and died in St James's Palace on 20 November, aged just fifty-four. The 'library' subsequently fell into disrepair.

Throughout the century, the park witnessed many military parades and manoeuvres, especially intense during the most critical periods of the War of Austrian Succession (1740–8). When the war was brought to an end through the Treaty of Aix-la-Chapelle, George II was to witness the spectacular celebrations in the park to commemorate this event from an ornate pavilion specially built near the Queen's Library. The building was called the 'Temple of Peace' and was designed by Monseigneur Cavalieri Servadoni, who had a significant reputation in Paris. The building would be fitted, at its centre, with a 'grand and extensive' musical gallery, above which would be an allegorical figure of Peace attended by the massive figures of Neptune and Mars. On a pole at the top was to be an illumination representing the sun, which was to burn, allegedly, almost throughout the night of festivities. Handel was chosen to compose a grand military overture, with over one hundred cannon fired from arcades in the Temple to provide the punctuation. Apart from the royal pavilion there were comfortable viewing galleries for the Privy Council, the House of Lords, the House of Commons, foreign diplomats and the dignitaries of the City of London, led by the Lord Mayor.

Beyond all these enclosures for the most privileged, great crowds of people milled about. All the park gates had been opened and there was a long gap in the wall facing Piccadilly to facilitate entrance. As soon as the King was in his place, the performance started with Handel's great overture, and the cannons firing when disaster struck. The Temple of Peace caught fire, and in the ensuing minutes Upper St James's Park became a scene of the most appalling confusion with many injuries and at least one fatality. With terrifying rapidity the entire area became engulfed in a series of fires and explosions as thousands of fireworks were prematurely set alight. Within the privileged enclosures, panic also set in, the galleries being flimsily built and ornately draped. Royalty was forced to retreat, which was just as well, as the Queen's Library also caught fire and was badly damaged. Sadly, the Temple of Peace had not lasted long.

Further changes were made to Upper St James's Park during the latter part of the eighteenth century. In 1767 the park was reduced in size by George III so that the gardens of Buckingham House could be enlarged, and after 1780 the park was used less and less by the military and increasingly for social gathering. Lower St James's Park had deteriorated considerably and the Upper Park was seen as more fashionable, particularly with the building of the new houses north of Piccadilly.

With the apparent ending of the Napoleonic Wars in the spring of 1814, the park was again chosen as one of the principal sites for national rejoicing. The beginning of August 1814 marked the centenary of the accession of the House of Hanover in Britain, so it was decided to combine the two celebrations, even though the Prince Regent was now so unpopular in

23

The building constructed in Green Park for the Royal
Fireworks on 27 April 1749, celebrating the signing
of the Treaty of Aix-la-Chapelle in 1748 (English,
eighteenth century). The music for the fireworks
was composed by G. F. Handel (1685–1759).

The revolving Temple of Concord illuminated, as erected in the park in celebration of the glorious peace of 1814. Originally published and produced by Edward Orme, London, 1814.

London that the streets had often to be cleared before he drove out from his palace at Carlton House. On this occasion, nearly a third of the park from Constitution Hill downwards was taken over and an imaginatively designed temporary building was to be the background for a grand pyrotechnic display. The building, designed by Sir William Congreve and plainly an emblem of war, was given the name 'The Temple of Concord', which suggested that some major transformation would take place in it before the celebrations were over. The entire structure slowly revolved so that the spectators could view all the scenes painted on the castle walls, which recalled the great heroes and triumphs of the British people, culminating in the victory over Napoleon. This was the first stage of the celebrations and was to be illuminated by the massed display of fireworks and the roar of cannon. On the very same evening, celebrations were under way in St James's Park, as described earlier (see pages 12–13), with elaborate celebrations designed by Nash featuring his Chinese pagoda and another firework display. At midnight, the great fortress in the Upper St James's Park revolved merrily

A peaceful scene along an avenue in Green Park.

Wellington Arch, also known as Constitution Arch or (originally) the Green Park Arch, is a triumphal arch located to the south of Hyde Park in central London and at the western corner of Green Park. Built nearby between 1826 and 1830 to a design by Decimus Burton, it was moved to its present position in 1882–3.

on its axis with a deafening roar, and the celebrations went off without mishap – unlike in nearby Lower St James's Park. Many of those attending the Upper Park celebrations went down to the Lower Park in order to witness the chaos and mayhem there.

By the early 1820s both Green Park and St James's Park had deteriorated to such an extent that the Commissioners of Woods, the officials responsible for them, issued a strong report urging radical changes, which coincided with the wish of George IV and the government that both parks should in

future be opened 'For the gratification and enjoyment of the Public'. In St James's Park this ultimately led to the Nash redevelopment. In Green Park the Commissioners suggested the planting of shrubberies along the northern and eastern boundaries together with new plantations of trees.

After the death of George IV, William IV showed little interest and Green Park was sadly neglected. In 1835 a writer in *The Original* complained bitterly about the disgraceful state into which the Green Park had been allowed to fall. There had been talk of terraced ornamental gardens being introduced to give beauty and grandeur to the vista across the park to the palace, as suggested by Sir Charles Barry, architect of the new Houses of Parliament, but nothing came of it. With the death of William, and with Queen Victoria now settled into Buckingham Palace, the Green Park was now well looked after within a landscape of trees, grass and paths. The Queen's Basin with its fountain had outlived its usefulness and was filled in. The decrepit Ranger's Lodge that had stood at the Hyde Park Corner end of the park was also demolished.

In the early years of Victoria's reign, a number of bizarre incidents occurred in or near the Green Park. In June 1838 the female balloonist

Canada Gate, commissioned in 1905 as part of the memorial to Queen Victoria (who had died in 1901) and presented to London by Canada.

Mrs Graham was engaged by the Government to make an ascent from the Green Park as part of the Queen's Coronation festivities. This, however, ended in tragedy when one of the balloon's grapnels tore a coping stone from the roof of a house in Marylebone Lane, which fell and fatally hit a passer-by. In June 1840 lunatic Edward Oxford fired two shots at the young Queen as she was driving past in her carriage with Prince Albert. A further attempt was made in May 1842 by another lunatic, named Francis, and yet another in 1849.

In essence, despite these traumatic and violent dramas throughout its history, the Green Park has quietly changed with the seasons. In 1889, the roadway at Constitution Hill was thrown open to the public as a thoroughfare for carriages, but limited to a number of specially favoured persons. In the early part of the twentieth century, the Broad Walk was given a more formal appearance as part of a vista from Piccadilly down through the park to the ornamental gates presented by the Dominion of Canada. These led to the gardens round the massive statue of Queen Victoria in front of Buckingham Palace unveiled by George V in 1911. The northern end of the vista was greatly enriched in 1921 when the magnificent iron gates that had stood guard over Devonshire House on the north side of Piccadilly were bought from the then Duke of Devonshire, who had sold the family town-house for redevelopment.

The Green Park that emerged from the nineteenth century and developed during the twentieth century is now a pleasantly uncluttered place, somewhat resembling a small expanse of countryside in the heart of a great capital city. Little has changed in the last century with only two additions: the Constance Fund fountain with Diana the naked huntress, positioned in 1954, and the Canadian War Memorial in 1994. These have not affected the atmosphere of the park and the only real hint of formality is provided by the Broad Walk and the ornamental iron gates at either end. It really is a park of simple beauty.

Above left:
Green Park, despite its lack of facilities like those of nearby St James's Park, is popular for its peaceful nature.

Above:
The Royal Parks, though providing peace and tranquillity for visitors, are places of work for the many Royal Parks gardeners employed across them all.

HYDE PARK:
A PARK FOR THE PEOPLE

HYDE PARK is the most English of Royal Parks. One can walk, lie on the grass, play games, take exercise, and engage in sport – which even includes rowing on the Serpentine. Hyde Park has been described as 'nature's own plan, London's heritage from the prehistoric forest which surrounded Londinium' as well as 'the greatest People's Park in Europe'. The 'lungs of London' are said to refer to the many parks and squares in London, conveying the idea of their importance to the well-being of its inhabitants. This phrase was first attributed to William Pitt (1708 –78), the Earl of Chatham, by Lord Windham in a speech in the House of Commons on 30 June 1808, during a debate on encroachment of buildings upon Hyde Park. Windham said, 'It was a saying of Lord Chatham, that the parks were the lungs of London…'.

Hyde Park's history began nearly five hundred years ago. On 1 July 1536, Henry VIII compelled the Convent of Westminster to hand over to him, 'with their whole assent, consent and agreement', certain lands, including Neyte, Ebury, Toddington and 'the syte, soyle, circuyte and procyncte of the manor of Hyde, with all the demayne lands, tenements, rents, meadowes and pastures of the said manor'. Henry was interested only in hunting and his own pleasures; nor did he hesitate to punish those who poached from him with the death penalty, but it is thanks to him that Hyde became Hyde Park: he enclosed it with palings, covering an area of 620 acres, extending nearly as far as where Kensington Palace currently stands.

Edward VI continued with the royal use of the park, entertaining foreign visitors there on diplomatic visits. Elizabeth I's reign saw further hunting in Hyde Park when in 1558 she invited the Duke of Anjou there to witness the sport. James I was also a great hunter and was a frequent visitor to Hyde Park with his favourite hounds, Jowler and Jewel, often refreshing himself in the Banqueting House at Whitehall.

However, it was not until the reign of Charles I that the people of London were allowed access into Hyde Park. In 1635, access had been permitted to a horse race, with general access following in 1637. An early

Opposite:
The introduction of flowers to the Royal Parks was an innovation of the Commissioners of the Board of Works in the late 1850s. Today, they are as popular as ever.

31

King Henry and Anne Boleyn Deer Shooting, William Powell Frith (1819–1909).

play, a comedy written by James Shirley, called *Hide Parke*, describes some of the activities prevalent at the time, including horse racing, foot racing and morris-dancing, with drinks supplied by milkmaids who cried 'Milk of a red cow!' King Charles I was often present at these festivities in Hyde Park.

During the years of the English Civil War, Parliament feared attack and passed a bill in March 1643 to build a strong earthen rampart, with bastions and redoubts, around the city of London. Hyde Park at this time extended eastward to the site where Hamilton Place now stands. At the northeast corner of the park there was a 'Court of Guard', which kept watch on people who looked dangerous to the Parliamentarians. Among their duties was the prevention of such incidents as occurred when, owing to the great shortage of fuel among the population, 'several unruly and disorderly persons have in a tumultuous and riotous manner, broken into Hyde Park and pulled down the pales, to destroy his Majesty's deer and wood there'.

On 27 November 1652 Parliament 'resolved that Hyde Park be sold for ready money', together with other properties of his late Majesty. Hyde Park was sold in three lots to Richard Wilcox, John Tracy (a merchant) and Anthony Dean (a shipbuilder) for a total of £17,071 6s 8d. The Park covered 621 acres and had eleven pools. The new owners charged local people admission and ensured the entrances were well guarded. Cromwell himself was a frequent user, probably to satisfy his love for horses, but on two occasions he almost lost his life, one occasion being an assassination attempt. The last years of the Commonwealth saw Hyde Park deteriorate considerably. It was not until the Restoration that it 'took on glorious colours'. The sale of Hyde Park was nullified by the courts of law and Charles II enclosed it with a brick wall and made it the open-air fashion centre of London. Approximately in the middle of the park (as it was at that time) was a cicrular paling called the 'Tour', or more generally the 'Ring', set in a square of trees, and it was here that the fashionable gathered to ride and to drive. The Ring stood on the highest part of the park above the pools and the Westbourne, where horses came to be refreshed.

Charles, like others before him, held many military reviews in the park. By 1665, the Great Plague had afflicted London. The Duke of Albermarle had taken his troops to Hyde Park and encamped them there to attempt to avoid the ravages of this horrendous disease.

By the time William and Mary were on the throne, Hyde Park was plagued by highwaymen. As many of the aristocracy now lived in the charming village of Kensington and had to cross Hyde Park at night to get home, this proved very inconvenient. William himself liked Kensington, and had bought the manor from the Earl of Nottingham to make it his palace. William's response was to have the road between St James's and Kensington Palace lit with three hundred oil lamps – the first instance of any road being lit – described as 'very grand and inconceivably magnificent'. The lamps were only ever used in winter as during the summer they were 'preserved for their Majesties' further service' in the woodyard at the palace. William was also the first monarch to introduce guards to patrol the park each night until 11 o'clock; these were doubled 'and marched to and fro all night' when William threw casino parties at the palace. By the end of the seventeenth century, there were still incidents in the park and by 1699 a guard house was built in the park itself, present until 1902. William and Mary were not great users of Hyde Park apart from attending reviews held there, which were frequent during their reign. By the time George I came to the throne in 1714,

Charles I created a circular track called the 'Ring', where members of the royal court could drive their carriages. The park was opened to the public in 1637 and it soon became a fashionable place to visit, particularly on May Day.

there were Jacobite rebellions all over the country and Hyde Park was turned several times into an armed camp during his reign. These were grim times for many soldiers: they would be shot for major military offences;for minor ones they were tied to trees and flogged, or made to run the gauntlet through Hyde and Green Parks. These many camps were a big attraction to the population of London, especially for the females. Duelling became a significant issue and licensing hours were set down for places of amusement, which were ordered to close at ten every evening. A fine avenue of walnut trees flanked the park on the west and in 1725 the Chelsea Waterworks Company was granted a licence to build a reservoir and engine-house to supply the west of London with water.

George II and Queen Caroline had a greater influence on Hyde Park, with the appropriation of 300 acres of it to make Kensington Gardens, along with the draining of the pools and the enlargement of the Westbourne to make the Serpentine. A dyke was constructed across the valley, damming the Westbourne and raising a mound at the southeastern end of Kensington Gardens, on top of which a small temple was placed. By 1733 the Serpentine was completed. The waterfall at the east end was added in 1820 and the stone bridge was built by John Rennie in 1826 to carry the newly built West Carriage Drive along the boundary between Hyde Park and Kensington Gardens, dividing the lake into the Serpentine (east) and the Long Water (west).

In 1737 the 'New King's Road' was finished, running parallel with King William's 'Lamp Road' on the south. The 'Lamp Road' is now the north side of Rotten Row (whose name is a corruption of *Route du Roi*), and the 'New King's Road' the other side. Sadly, newspapers in December 1736 reported: 'The Ring in Hyde Park being quite disused by the quality and gentry, we hear that the ground will be taken in for enlarging the Kensington Gardens'. As Kensington Gardens was extended and improved, Hyde Park was deteriorating. Robberies were rife, Walpole himself being held up in November 1749, resulting in many more hangings at Tyburn. However, it was during the reign of George III that Hyde Park became notorious in for duels (no fewer than 172 were fought, with many fatalities) along with almost daily robberies. A bell used to ring periodically during the evenings in Kensington to muster those who wanted to return to London, so that they could cross in groups for their mutual protection.

The severe winters of 1767 and 1784 saw skating on the Serpentine, with the Prince of Wales one of the many spectators. Riding and driving along Rotten Row had become the new fashion towards the end of the eighteenth century, with an array of carriages. Militray manoeuvres were still commonplace at the beginning of the nineteenth century, with 'seven tons of powder a week … consumed in practices…' In the last days of

George III, Hyde Park was described as comfortless and bleak, and likened by Byron to 'a vegetable puncheon Call'd Park, where there is neither fruit nor flower Enough to gratify a bee's slight munching'. On Thursday 19 July 1821, George IV was crowned and for the first time in its history coronation celebrations were held in Hyde Park; the south side of the park was used for the festivities, with a boat race on the Serpentine used for a boat race and tents and marquees erected at the Ring. The park was open to all and huge crowds gathered in the evening for a lavish fireworks display. When the gate had to be closed to stem the enormous flow of people, ladders were erected over the palings and in many areas they were simply ripped out! 'The Serpentine and its banks were turned into a riot of merriment ... the water itself covered with boats ... and all classes joined in the sport of roundabouts and swings, witnessing also a spectacle on a stage near the cascade.'

In 1822 the Achilles statue was erected. The cost of £10,000 was donated by British women who had been eager to have a cast of a Greek statue found among Roman ruins in Italy. They had come to the conclusion that no finer

The fleet on the Serpentine river, commemorative of the Battle of the Nile, Au[gu]st. 1st, 1814. A mock naval battle between the English and French fleets, under American colours. Originally published and produced by Edward Orme, London, 1814.

The view of the fair in Hyde Park, Aug[us]t. 1st 1814. Originally published and produced by Edward Orme, London, 1814.

Opposite, top: Ionic screen, 1826–9, by Decimus Burton, commissioned by the Office of Woods to replace earlier wooden gates. The fluted Ionic screen and entablature are in Portland stone, embellished with friezes by John Henning in imitation of the Elgin Marbles.

tribute could be paid to the Duke of Wellington than to erect such a subject in his honour, in 'his own beloved Hyde Park'. The bronze came from cannons captured in military campaigns by the Iron Duke at Salamanca, Vittoria, Toulouse and Waterloo. This was London's first public nude statue since antiquity and despite its fig leaf it was still controversial. The English public, many of whom had never seen a nude statue before, abandoned Wellington Drive, retreating before his 'Disgrace' into Rotten Row and the Ladies' Mile.

A number of improvements were made to Hyde Park during George IV's reign by Decimus Burton, including a new bridge over the Serpentine. All roads and drives were improved and an extended 'Ring', nearly encircling the park, provided excellent facilities for the growing number of carriage folk who used it to recognise and be recognised, to envy or be envied. Charles II's brick wall was pulled down and new iron railings were substituted, while new gates and lodges were built at the Cumberland, Grosvenor, Stanhope and Hyde Park Corner gates. A new drive round Buck Hill and along the left bank of the Serpentine was also laid out. Decimus Burton's beautiful screen of fluted Ionic columns with Henning's frieze was built in 1827 — one of the most graceful but grand entrances to any park.

For the coronation of the Duke of Clarence as King William IV there were few festivities in Hyde Park and royal use of the park during his reign

Below left: *Making Decent*, cartoon showing William Wilberforce (1759–1833) covering up the statue of Achilles at Hyde Park Corner by Richard Westmacott (1775–1856). Published 1822 (litho), English school.

Below: The statue of Achilles today appears little changed.

was limited to simply driving around the Serpentine. This was soon to change when Victoria, who had been brought up mainly at Kensington Palace, became Queen. Hyde Park (which she loved) became the stage of many historic events throughout her reign. On 28 June 1838 Victoria was crowned, and a great Coronation Fair was held in Hyde Park between

37

'Male and Female
Macaronies; a
chapter heading
from Jacob
Larwood's *Story of
the London Parks*.'

the Serpentine and Park Lane. 'Fat boys were exhibited, and living skeletons, Irish giants and Welsh dwarfs, children fortunate in having two heads, animals with none. Conjurer, athlete, strong man, clown – all did their tricks in admiration of the coin which bore the young Queen's head.'

The Queen herself attended these festivities in the 'People's Hyde Park' and was given a great ovation. The Queen married Albert and ultimately moved to Buckingham Palace but it was the attempted murderous attack by Edward Oxford on 10 June 1840 at Constitution Hill that endeared her to the British people. The day after the attempt, Victoria and Albert drove in Hyde Park amid public cheers. They would drive every evening in Hyde Park between five and seven 'without pomp and drawn swords'. Rotten Row became a place of great etiquette, where it was now taboo to be vulgar, be drunk or even to smoke, as it 'offended the new frail sex'.

It was, however, the Great Exhibition that was to have the greatest impact on Hyde Park throughout its history. The purpose of the Great Exhibition

General view of the exterior of Crystal Palace, Hyde Park. Taken from Dickinson's comprehensive pictures of the Great Exhibition of 1851. Originally published in 1854.

General view
of the Albert
Memorial, the
monument to the
Prince Consort,
which occupies
part of the site
where the Crystal
Palace once stood.

was to bring the world to London, to show them Britain's material and spiritual greatness next to its own, to trade Britain's goods, and herald a Peace based on world prosperity and exchange. Several sites had been considered, including Regent's Park, Trafalgar Square and Leicester Square, but Albert's suggestion of the south side of Hyde Park was accepted. The Great Exhibition, held in the Crystal Palace designed by Joseph Paxton, met every conceivable type of opposition, as the building was erected over Rotten Row.

The glass structure, 1,851 feet in length, was opened on 1 May 1851 and the Prince Consort in his opening address accurately described the Crystal Palace as 'a building entirely novel in its construction ... and capable of containing 40,000 visitors, and affording a frontage for the exhibition of goods to the extent of more than ten miles'. In reality, as many as 100,000 people at a time visited the Exhibition. With over 15,000 exhibitors, it was open for 141 days with a total of more than six million visitors. Queen Victoria was 'quite beaten' by the vast glass miracle, 'and my head bewildered,

from the myriads of beautiful and wonderful things, which now quite dazzle one's eyes!' The palace was moved piece by piece to Sydenham in south London when the exhibition eventually closed. To commemorate it, the Albert Memorial was built in Kensington Gardens, immediately after the Exhibition.

The 1850s also saw the relocation of Nash's Marble Arch from the front of Buckingham Palace to Hyde Park. It was rebuilt by Thomas Cubitt as a ceremonial entrance to the northeast corner of Hyde Park at Cumberland Gate, although it is now separated from the park by a busy road.

Riding on Rotten Row was as popular as ever but the divisions between class and sex were very apparent. The fashionable world made Hyde Park, now embellished since 1860 with flowers, the place to be. The 1890s saw ladies turning out in droves on bicycles, with the police 'terrified of their speed'.

During the latter part of Victoria's reign, more and more of the working classes were now using Hyde Park, as London grew and the countryside

The design of Nash's Marble Arch is based on that of the Arch of Constantine in Rome and the Arc de Triomphe du Carrousel in Paris. It was originally intended to carry a series of sculpture celebrating British victories during the Napoleonic Wars. It now stands in a peculiar location in the middle of a traffic island.

Skating on
the Serpentine
in 1895.

was becoming more distant. The fairs at the beginning of the century had
been important in changing the public attitude towards Hyde Park, and in
revealing it as a place where one could take one's food and picnic, and even
skate on the Serpentine during cold winters.

Police waiting for
the Reform
Meeting, *Illustrated
London News,*
May 1867.

   It was during this time that Hyde Park gradually became a forum for the
people. On 24 June 1855 oratory came to Hyde Park. A meeting was publicly
announced, to be held at 3 p.m., to protest against Lord Robert Grosvenor's

Sunday Trading Bill. Despite efforts to prevent this, democracy took up the challenge and by 2.30 p.m. about 150,000 people had assembled in Hyde Park, including Karl Marx: an orator began to speak, with the crowd barracking the wealthy promenaders of Rotten Row with shouts of 'Go to Church'. Despite the police attempting to arrest the orator, he got away and a battle ensued. Next day, however, Lord Robert withdrew the Bill. On Sunday 14 October about five thousand people gathered in Hyde Park and were addressed by 'a man of serious aspect' about the high price of bread. These were the beginnings of regular meetings, some of which ended in riots, including one in which 'partisans both of Garibaldi and of the Pope arrived in Hyde Park, to the extent of eighty or ninety thousand on both sides. About four hundred police were there to keep them in order.' In 1866 the Reform League attempted a meeting, which again, despite the presence of 1,700 police and the closure of all the park gates, resulted in two days of rioting. With the growth of trade unions, demonstrations ultimately became quieter. A mosaic laid in 2000 commemorates a tree burnt down during the Reform League riots in 1866. The stump became a focal point for

Grenadier Guards waiting for the Reform Meeting; a contemporary engraving from the *Illustrated London News*, 18 May 1867.

43

Rima, the Hyde Park 'atrocity'.

The world-famous Rotten Row, the place to be and be seen, in its heyday at the dawn of the twentieth century.

meetings and notices. Continued attempts by the authorities to stop them led directly to the creation of Speakers' Corner in 1872.

The dawn of the twentieth century brought a great transformation for Hyde Park and as early as 1906 'motor landaulettes and hansoms first plied at Hyde Park Corner'. George V was an early morning devotee of Rotten Row. During the darkest days of the First World War, American troops in London would also frequently parade through the park.

In a secluded corner of Hyde Park now sits a striking monument to the novelist, naturalist and ornithologist W. H. Hudson. The sense of rustic diversion and the tranquillity of the bird sanctuary that surrounds the memorial may today seem apt, but when it was first unveiled in 1925 Hudson's memorial caused great controversy. The man chosen to carve the monument to Hudson was Jacob Epstein. It was a bold choice to say the least, as his forays into public sculpture had already ruffled a few feathers within the art establishment. Epstein threw himself into the task. According to Epstein himself, the finished relief panel drew 'gasps of horror' in May 1925 when the Prime Minister, Stanley Baldwin, drew back the curtain. To the assembled throng the sculpture

In 2010 Tory MPs Edward Leigh and Desmond Swayne, furious at being prevented from getting to the water during a spell of freezing weather, tabled questions in the House of Commons demanding to know why the historic access had been denied. (A pair of Tory MPs had thus succeeded in preserving their freedom to swim in a lido commissioned by George Lansbury – renowned pre-war socialist and future leader of the Labour Party.)

Hyde Park still has a fleet of rowing boats (now supplemented by pedal boats), which operate on the famous Serpentine; also Britain's first Solarshuttle. This magnificent vessel glides silently across the lake, powered only by the sun.

45

A detail of the Cavalry Memorial, sculpted by Adrian Jones in 1924, uses bronze cast from guns captured in the First World War.

seemed like an awkwardly carved figure of a distorted and explicitly nude girl surrounded by grotesque birds. A media campaign followed in which the *Morning Post* described *Rima* – or 'the Hyde Park Atrocity' as it was quickly dubbed – as 'Mr Epstein's nightmare in stone', and the sculptor as 'the most famous example of a great sculptor who has sold his soul to the devil'.

In the spring of 1930, Hyde Park took on a new phase, as for over two hundred years there had been no swimming allowed in the Serpentine, except in the early mornings, and this had been restricted to men and boys. George Lansbury, the first Commissioner of Works, set out to make Hyde Park a more cheerful place for young and old, men and

The Bandstand, popular in Victorian times and still today.

women alike. Bathing establishments were erected on the Serpentine and became known as 'Lansbury's Lido', enabling Londoners to bathe at all times of the day; he also opened the Serpentine for the first time to women.

London's greatest 'green lung' continues to prosper and evolve, but not without controversy. The Queen Elizabeth Gates, just to the east, are amongst the latest additions to the park, installed in 1993 in honour of the Queen Mother. Their sculptor, Giuseppe Lund, designed them to be 'feminine and fresh with the charm of an English garden', but they have since been described by critics as 'appalling ... a music hall joke, a pantomime dame, and a seaside postcard rolled into one'.

Further controversy ensued with the installation of the Diana, Princess of Wales Memorial Fountain, a memorial dedicated to the princess, who died in a car crash in 1997. It was designed to express Diana's spirit and love of children and was opened in July 2004. Diana was seen as a contemporary and accessible princess, so the goal of the memorial fountain was to allow people to access the structure and the water for quiet wading and

The Queen Elizabeth Gates, installed in honour of the Queen Mother in 1993. Lord Rogers described the design as 'romantic candyfloss' and compared it to one of the Queen Mother's hats. Even her grandson Viscount Linley said he 'absolutely loathed' it.

contemplation. However, shortly after its opening and after three hospitalisations caused by people slipping in the water, the fountain was closed. It reopened in August 2004, surrounded by a new fence, and people were prevented from walking or running in the water by six wardens. Now, however, entering the water is again permitted. Even though the fountain was open only for a part of the 2004 season, and the weather was not particularly wet, the grass adjacent to part of the fountain was badly damaged, and it appeared that it would turn to a quagmire if heavy rain ever fell during the main visiting season. Thus, in December 2004, another alteration project was started. This involved work on the drainage, together with laying new hard surfaces on some of the most frequently walked areas of the site and the planting of a special hard-wearing rye grass mix in others.

Hyde Park has continued to be enjoyed by the masses throughout the twentieth century and into the twenty-first century. Hyde Park has hosted Orwell, Lenin and Marx, and more recently Bruce Springsteen and Bon Jovi. A park for mass celebrations since VE Day, and to public events including Proms in the Park, it was host to some 2012 Olympic events and has held countless music festivals, despite restrictions placed on their number in 2012.

Bruce Springsteen performing in Hyde Park, Hard Rock Calling, 2009.

An inviting set of deck chairs welcomes visitors with an opportunity to soak up the sun.

The Diana, Princess of Wales Memorial Fountain.

KENSINGTON GARDENS: A ROYAL PARK WITH A ROYAL PALACE

THE JOINT REIGN of William and Mary saw major changes in nearby Hyde Park, foreshadowing its future development, but it was the hiving-off of Kensington Gardens that had the greatest impact. William's ill health and chronic asthma brought him and Mary to Kensington. The damp air and mists of the nearby Thames, with pollution from the smoke from tens of thousands of chimneys, had made him seriously ill. In 1689 he was persuaded to recuperate at Hampton Court, close to the river but where the air was known to be fresh and clean. But William needed a place close to Whitehall that was healthy and invigorating and it was to Kensington that he turned. The Earl of Nottingham, one of his most loyal servants, had inherited a Jacobean mansion on the western edge of Hyde Park in the village of Kensington. William bought it from Nottingham in July 1689 and immediately set about improving it. Ironically, it was left to Mary to supervise as William was frequently in Europe organising alliances against the French or leading armies against them. Mary took on the task with vigour and enthusiasm, visiting almost daily, and they moved in just before Christmas.

William needed a safe route from Kensington to Whitehall and in 1690 a wide road was laid out which ran from his new home, then known as Kensington House, along the southern boundary of Hyde Park, then to Constitution Hill, past Green Park and on to St James's Palace and Horse Guards Parade – the *Route de Roi* that became Rotten Row. The task of laying out the gardens was given to Henry Wise and George London of Brompton Nurseries.

William was a keen gardener and his designs reflected his Dutch background, so inevitably Kensington House was laid out very formally with a central feature of a broad tree-lined avenue which ran down from the terrace in front of the King's Gallery. On either side were formal parterres planted with dwarf trees set in designs of box, often circular but also arabesque. The gardens were extensive and covered at the time up to 26 acres. Already some of Hyde Park had been taken in, a forerunner of further encroachments. Even after the fire of 1691, works continued and

Opposite:
The Sunken Gardens at Kensington Park. These have changed little in the last century, as can be seen on page 59.

51

Mary was happy at Kensington. Her happiness was short-lived, however; sadly she died at the age of thirty-two, having caught smallpox, and left William devastated (he lived until 1702).

His successor, Queen Anne, and her husband Prince George of Denmark, moved into Kensington, and she immediately set to work on the gardens, employing Henry Wise, thus making him the most sought-after gardener in the country. Her changes were significant and her dislike of William's formal Dutch gardens resulted in their uprooting and replacement by a formal garden designed by Wise. It was no secret that Anne and William had never been on good terms. Undoubtedly the most important development was her enclosure of no less than 100 acres of Hyde Park to make a paddock for herds of deer and antelope. The gravel pits behind the house were planted with trees and made into a much-admired garden. Further improvements included the Orangery designed by Hawksmoor and Vanbrugh, which became Anne's 'Summer Supper House'. Anne's last few years brought her little happiness. George died in 1708 and Anne spent many of her hours driving herself round the gardens, and frequently the paddock, as she had been a keen huntress in her younger days. Anne died in Kensington House on 1 August 1714, thus beginning the rule of the House of Hanover.

George I was fifty-four when he came to England, having lived in the palace of Herrenhausen, in Hanover. Its delightful gardens reflected in a more modest way the glories of Versailles, with formal avenues lined with trees, statues of amorous fauns and dryads, fountains and waterfalls. When George

The Royal Palace of Kensington in the reign of William III.

The Royal Palace of KINGSINGTON.

eventually came to Kensington, his main concern there was to extend the house into a palace and embellish the main apartments. For years he left the gardens very much as they were. He had a modest rectangular basin constructed, where his turtles could swim, and a 'snailery'. In Queen Anne's paddock was a menagerie of tigers and civets. Water supply was an issue until the Chelsea Water Company was given permission to build a large reservoir in the Walnut Avenue in Hyde Park and pipe a supply to the palace. By now, George had begun to turn his attention to the gardens and parkland beyond. In 1726 he approved an ambitious plan that had been prepared by the Royal Gardener, Henry Wise, with his assistant, Charles Bridgeman, who was an exponent of the new 'natural' style of landscaping soon to dominate the English scene. Significant preparatory work was carried out in 1727, but George died before he could see the gardens completed. Queen Caroline, wife of George II, however, enthusiastically implemented and extended the new developments, forming the framework of Kensington Gardens, which still remains today.

Another 200 acres were taken in from Hyde Park, and Charles Bridgeman was now solely in charge of works, employed between 1728 and 1738. The formal gardens south of the palace were turned into lawns. Queen Anne's avenue running from Bayswater to Kensington was widened to 50 feet to make 'The Broad Walk' and was lined with elms. The most significant works, however, were about to unfold. First, the large octagonal 'basin' (later the Round Pond), set in a semicircle of lawns and trees, with the eye guided to the enchanting Long Water and Serpentine by three great tree-lined avenues in *patte d'oie* style, was created out of the ponds of the Westbourne. Beyond were uninterrupted vistas of the wooded landscape of Hyde Park, and instead of the usual boundary wall or pales there was a ha-ha (a deep fosse or ditch). Bridgeman had created a park designed for civilised men and women where they could walk and admire this elegant scene. A curious introduction completed in 1733 was a 'garden mount', built to a height of 150 feet, surrounded by a grove of trees and surmounted by a revolving summerhouse which enabled Queen Caroline and members of the court to enjoy looking down and around the splendid view. Below were her fine new tree-lined avenues, interspersed with copses and winding paths designed in the rococo style by William Kent, who in addition to the summerhouse on the mount also built 'the Queen's Temple'. The greatest view must have been to the east – the gracefully shaped expanse of the Long Water and the Serpentine. Her plans were even more ambitious, including the building of a grandiose palace in Hyde Park and the closure of Hyde Park to the public, but were never realised. By the time of Caroline's death in 1737, the new gardens of Kensington Palace were well established and they were opened as a privilege to a limited public on Saturdays if the court was elsewhere such as

Richmond. Gatekeepers were instructed to admit only those whose dress and deportment belonged to the upper and middle classes. Soldiers, sailors, servants and those poorly dressed were excluded and as a result would gather outside the gardens, loudly mocking those who had been admitted.

George II outlived Caroline by twenty-three years and Kensington gradually declined, although the gardens were kept in reasonable order. He died in 1760 and was the last reigning monarch who resided at Kensington. His successor, George III, lived at St James's Palace and was in the process of buying Buckingham House. By the nineteenth century Kensington Gardens were opened daily to the 'respectably dressed'.

Queen Caroline's mount was levelled, the ha-ha gradually filled in and ornamental trees and shrubs planted on the west bank

An entrance to Kensington Palace and Gardens during the Regency, attributed to Her Royal Highness Princess Sophia.

A Scene in Kensington Gardens. or. Fashions and Frights of 1829.

'A scene in Kensington Gardens, or fashion and frights of 1829'. An amusing sketch showing people dressed up in the park. George Cruikshank, 1828.

of the Long Water, but most significant was the laying out of the Flower Walk, which stretches for nearly a mile and was a sight to behold. Sheep were brought in to impart a sense of rural tranquillity. However, London was growing at such a phenomenal rate that developers were beginning to run out of building sites around Hyde Park, began to move westwards to the environs of Kensington Gardens. In the 1840s a number of sites along the western boundary of the palace were leased for villas; these were significant buildings, now mainly embassies, with a very grand private road lined with noble trees. These villas brought a whole new community of extremely rich tenants who soon pressed for and obtained special privileges, including private entrances to the Gardens, ultimately leading to the replacement of the old walls with open iron railings. Development continued around Kensington in the south and along the Bayswater Road in the north with new squares, terraces and crescents and new shopping areas along Kensington High Street and in Notting Hill Gate.

The Victorian age saw a greater emphasis on the importance of children; nannies and nursemaids were often seen parading with well-nurtured children in perambulators, especially near the Round Pond. Further boundary walls were replaced with railings and more entrances created; public lavatories and then tea rooms were built; statues and the Albert Memorial were erected and installed to commemorate the great and the good. The statue of J. M. Barrie's Peter Pan stands on a pedestal by

Kensington Palace. For a royal residence in the age of Louis XIV it is surprisingly modest in scale with only two grand façades and the rest comprising buildings assembled around three courtyards. Despite being designed by Sir Christopher Wren, its restrained style is close to contemporary Dutch architecture.

The Kensington Gardens flower gardens – the poet Thomas Tickell (1685–1740) described them thus: 'Where Kensington, luxuriant in her bowers, Sees snow of blossoms, and a wild of flowers.'

the Long Water, decorated with squirrels, rabbits and mice. Over in the children's playground is the Elfin Oak, a stump from Richmond Park, carved by Ivor Innes in the 1930s with fairies, elves and pet animals. Dutch elm disease took its toll in the 1950s and sadly the great avenues planted by Queen Caroline were lost, to be replaced with lime and maples – the public outcry was nevertheless relentless. The Flower Walk continued to be a haven of peace and tranquillity in Victorian and Edwardian times. But despite Victoria's childhood at Kensington Palace and having grown up in and around the Gardens, she would never go back to Kensington Gardens. There is, however, a statue of her in front of Kensington Palace, looking out across the Broad Walk and the Round Pond, where she played as a child, celebrating the first fifty years of her life. It is a statue of her as a young

Queen Anne's avenue running from Bayswater to Kensington was widened to 50 feet to make 'The Broad Walk' and was lined with elms. The Queen Victoria statue in marble was sculpted in 1893 by Princess Louise, Duchess of Argyll, and presented by the Kensington Golden Jubilee Memorial Executive Committee. The young queen is wearing coronation robes.

woman upon her new throne, and is fitting, both because Kensington Gardens is the park of her childhood, and because the statue was sculpted by Princess Louise, one of her children.

Like many of the other Royal Parks, Kensington Gardens has evolved gently and peacefully into the twentieth century and beyond. Unlike its busy and bustling neighbour, Hyde Park, Kensington Gardens has a smaller number of monuments and statues. It was perhaps best known for the huge outpouring of public grief when Diana, Princess of Wales was tragically killed in 1997. She was a resident of Kensington Palace and as a consequence, thousands of people left public offerings of flowers, candles, cards and personal messages outside Kensington Palace for many months. A huge wooden pirate ship is now the amazing centrepiece of the Diana, Princess of Wales' Memorial Playground. This children's wonderland opened on 30 June 2000, in memory of the late princess. Located next to her Kensington Palace home, the playground is a fitting tribute for a princess who loved the innocence of childhood.

The Serpentine Gallery was built as a refreshment room in 1934 but now displays Arts Council exhibitions of contemporary art. In 2013 it was the subject of a major new expansion. The new Serpentine Gallery Pavilion has been designed and built by multi-award-winning Japanese architect Sou Fujimoto. This intricate and unusually latticed structure of 20-mm steel poles has a lightweight and semi-transparent appearance so that it blends into the landscape and contrasts with the classical backdrop of the Gallery's

The Italian Garden was the ideas of Prince Albert, who commissioned landscape designer Sir James Pennethorne (1801–71) to design the layout. Sir Charles Barry and Robert Richardson Banks designed the ornate pump house; and John Thomas (1813–62) was responsible for all the reliefs and sculptures apart from William Calder Marshall's *Jenner*, which was 'inaugurated by Prince Albert, and the first to be erected in Kensington Gardens in 1862'.

The Serpentine
Pavilion (2013),
designed by
Japanese architect
Sou Fujimoto.

colonnaded east wing. This complements as well as contrasts with the magnificent Orangery built in 1704–5 to a design by Nicholas Hawksmoor, later altered by Vanbrugh, and used for summer supper parties. It is now a very popular restaurant.

Today, Kensington Gardens is particularly popular for sunbathing and picnics in fine weather, and provides a healthy walking route to work for commuters heading into the city, as well as being used extensively by joggers and runners. The importance of the historic landscape and the desire to maintain its primary role as a peaceful refuge for people living in, working in or visiting central London are its chief characteristics.

The Sunken Gardens at the turn of the twentieth century.

The Pump House and Italian Gardens – the purpose of the Pump House was to raise and supply water to the head of the Long Water.

THE REGENT'S PARK:
A ROYAL PARTNERSHIP

IN *GEORGIAN LONDON* by John Summerson, the author describes Regent's Park: 'Once and only once has a great plan for London, affecting the capital as a whole, been projected and carried to completion.' It was the boldness of the Prince Regent, later King George IV, creating his own most lasting memorial, and the genius of John Nash, which saw this 'great plan for London' realised. Yet its history precedes Georgian times, like many of the Royal Parks of London. The Marylebone Park Crown Estate, from which Regent's Park was developed, was originally part of the Great Forest of Middlesex – a region dominated by 'wooded glades and lairs of wild beasts, deer both red and fallow, wild bulls and boars'. Most of the land lay in the Manor of Tyburn, which during the Middle Ages was held by the Abbess of Barking, on behalf of the Crown. Taken over by Henry VIII when he dissolved the monasteries in 1536, he enclosed a roughly circular area, realising it would make an excellent extension to his game preserves. Marylebone Park, his new park, was surrounded by a deep ditch and embankment, with lodges constructed in which his gamekeepers could live. Successive monarchs would enjoy the chase in Marylebone Park, including Edward VI, who had the whole park fenced. Despite Mary Tudor's attempts to break up the parks of Marylebone and Hyde, her sister, Elizabeth I, ensured the park was preserved and anyone found poaching was severely punished.

Radical changes occurred during the reign of Charles I, with clearance of trees and brushwood to provide fuel for the poor citizens of London. After the English Civil War, Cromwell found himself short of available money and within days of the King's execution an Act of Parliament was passed that authorised the sale of the royal estates. Marylebone Park was sold to three cavalry officers in Cromwell's army, who paid little more than £13,000 for it. The new owners immediately set about cutting down many of its ancient trees in an attempt to recover as quickly as possible the money they had paid for the land and to show, if they could, some kind of profit. By the time Charles II had returned from exile, few of the thousands of splendid oaks, elms and limes that had stood so majestically in Marylebone Park

Opposite:
The Avenue Gardens in full bloom and fully restored.

A dairy farm in
Marylebone Park
in 1750.

remained. What remained of the park was taken back into royal ownership and new tenants proceeded to plough up most of the ground or use it for dairy farming.

By the middle of the eighteenth century, Marylebone Park was providing an ever-expanding London with a fair part of the hay for its mews and stables as well as its daily quotas of milk. The fence that enclosed the former royal hunting ground had also virtually disappeared. It was the Surveyor General of the Crown Lands, John Fordyce, appointed in 1793, who saw the potential in the now denuded Marylebone Park. It was now very much a pastoral landscape, with a number of public houses, farms and cottages. Along the southern boundary of the park was the New Road, which had been laid down in 1757 to connect Islington and Paddington and acted as London's first by-pass. On taking up his appointment, Fordyce had to decide whether to sanction a request made by the Duke of Portland to lay down a new turnpike road through Marylebone Park. The Duke's intentions were purely altruistic – a new church was needed for the people of Marylebone, and he had offered to give some of his land for it, provided that an access road could be made over royal ground. Fordyce was incredibly shrewd, as well as astute; he was well aware of the enormous fortunes being made by others who were exploiting the land they were fortunate enough to own in the immediate vicinity of the capital. In essence, he recognised the true worth of Marylebone Park, and that the new turnpike road would significantly 'lessen the value of the Ground for building to such a degree as no price or value that could be expected to be given to the Crown, for the Land desired, would be found sufficient to compensate'. Fordyce therefore ensured that the Duke's proposals were refused.

Fordyce was keen to progress with the development of the park; he had it fully surveyed and suggested that a public competition should be held, so that the very best development ideas might be brought forward. Plans were sent to several leading architects but, despite the offer of £1,000 to the winning entry, the response was disappointing. Only Portland's surveyor, John White, showed any interest, and as he lived in the park, this was hardly surprising. He was loath to lose its pleasant rural character and his entry bore no resemblance to what Fordyce envisaged. White's plan proposed a roughly circular ring of villas, each standing in its own grounds, built on the perimeter of the park, the centre being kept as a pastoral pleasure ground, complete with a serpentine lake. His proposals also included a splendid crescent at the southern end of the park, near the New Road, an idea picked up eventually by later planners.

Five years later, and enter a 'thick, squat, dwarf figure, with round head, snub nose and little eyes' called John Nash, who was already closely associated with the Prince of Wales – Nash's wife, Mary Anne Bradley, was alleged to be the mistress of the Prince. Whether or not this was true, the association was to have a significant impact on the future of Marylebone Park, as the Prince was especially interested in architecture. Nash had spent

Plan of improvements proposed for Marylebone Park in 1809 by John White, with housing round its perimeter. White's design influenced Nash's own ideas although White was never acknowledged by Nash.

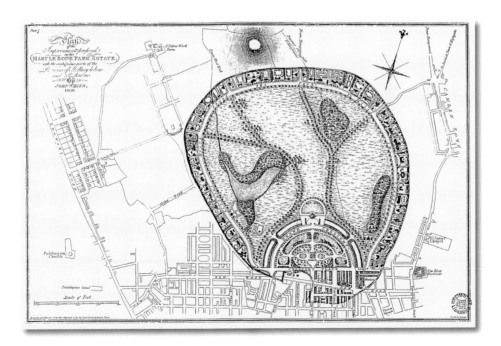

his maturity in designing country houses, chiefly in Wales, and had a friendly relationship with a group of landowners there, including Richard Payne Knight and Sir Uvedale Price. It was these two gentlemen who had evolved the theory of the 'picturesque' and had applied it to the buildings on their own estates. They believed in the supremacy of the natural, the romantic and the picturesque over all the other types of beauty, and that buildings should be related to the landscape in which they stood. The greatest exponent of their theories was landscape gardener Humphry Repton, who endeavoured not to regulate nature, but to release the latent possibilities in the grounds of the country estates where he was employed. Repton and Nash worked in partnership between 1795 and 1802, and from him Nash learnt a great deal. Nash closely examined Fordyce's recommendations, which stated:

> Distance is best computed by time; and if means could be found to lessen the time going from Marylebone to the Houses of Parliament, the value of the ground for building would be thereby proportionately increased. The best, and probably upon the whole, the most advantageous way of doing that, would be by opening a great street from Charing-Cross towards a central part of Marylebone Park.

Portrait of John Nash (1827) at the age of seventy-two by Thomas Lawrence.

Sadly, Fordyce died two months after the report was published. The idea of a competition had by now been abandoned and instead surveyors Thomas Chawner and Thomas Leverton and architects John Nash and his assistant James Morgan were instructed to come up with plans. Leverton and Chawner's plans were at best dull and uninspiring: left to them, Marylebone Park would have been a stark network of straight streets and rectangular squares, unrelieved by any curves, and would simply have been an extension of the Portland Estate just to the south. The Commissioners were saved from this depressing option by the romantic genius of John Nash. Encouraged by the Prince Regent, Nash was ready to indulge in some *folie de grandeur*. Nash took up Fordyce's idea that a new road should be provided, creating a link to the centre of London, a *Via Triumphalis* that would lead from the Prince's sumptuous home at Carlton House, to a superb country villa somewhere near the middle of the park, with Portland Place as the starting place for the road. Nash's plans for the park were ambitious – he declared: 'The attraction of open Space, free air and the scenery of Nature, with the means and invitation of exercise on horseback, on foot and in Carriages, shall be preserved or created in Mary-le-bone Park, as allurements or motives for the wealthy part of the Public to establish themselves there…'

The park, in essence, was to become an exclusive and self-contained residential area, in which a relatively small number of rather splendid villas would be built. These would be placed in such a way that

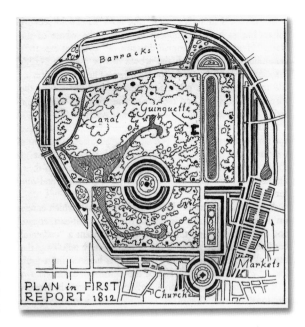

Engraving of John Nash's plan of Marylebone Park appended to the Commissioner's First Report to Parliament, 4 June 1812, and ordered to be printed by the House of Commons, 13 June 1812, by John Nash.

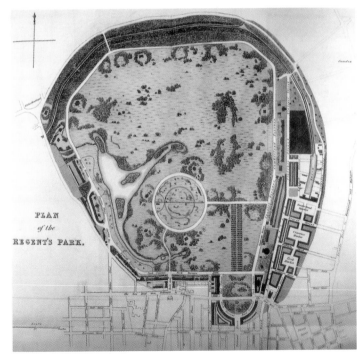

A later plan by Nash amended in 1826, in which the barracks has moved to Albany Street and the entrance to the park is no longer a circus, and there are now fewer villas in the park.

Holford House, c. 1835, the last of the villas to be built in the park, was the largest and most expensive. It was designed by Decimus Burton for the wine merchant James Holford. Badly bombed during the Second World War, it was subsequently demolished.

each would have open views over the park but would still be invisible from the others. Nash's vision included shops, markets and other conveniences. Tradesmen would be encouraged to settle there in small houses, although not where they could be seen from the more desirable residences in the park. Nash's design was revolutionary, although, despite the Prince Regent's backing, changes were enforced on him by the Commissioners. The number of villas was reduced from fifty-six to twenty-six. The canal that he had proposed to run across the park was to run just inside the perimeter to the north. Other changes were forced on a forever grumbling Nash. However, with the authorisation to proceed, Nash set to work with immense energy and vigour; he needed plenty of both, as work did not progress smoothly. He began by laying out roads and plantations but ran into trouble with local landowners in relation to the construction of the Regent's Canal; the locals believed that the stagnant waters would be a constant danger to health. Next, Charles Mayor, a business associate of Nash, who had taken up a number of leases, went bankrupt, owing £22,000. Nash struggled with rising prices and shortage of money, as Britain was engaged in a bitter war with France. Nash never lost faith but had to continually justify himself to the Commissioners. Despite these problems, the Prince Regent maintained his support and between 1819 and 1826 Nash's fortunes picked up. Terraces started to appear and ring the park, a handsome crescent was constructed, as well as a square, barracks, church and residential estates. By now King George IV had become obsessed with his new project at Buckingham Palace, where Nash was also engaged. As a result, the pavilion or even a mere *guinguette* was quietly forgotten. Of all the original villas, only a few were actually built, including St John's Lodge and The Holme, constructed for James Burton, the wealthy builder, who had come to Nash's aid when he was in serious financial difficulties. Designer of the villa was Decimus Burton, his tenth son, who

Cambridge Terrace and the Colosseum, originally built in 1825 by Richard Mott, who also built Chester Gate and Gloucester Terrace.

had a major part to play not only in designing many of the buildings and terraces in and around Regent's Park, but in many of London's other Royal Parks.

St Dunstan's Villa was another Decimus Burton commission. Other villas followed and included Hanover Lodge and South Villa in 1827. Despite the progress, John Nash aroused vociferous criticism. Nash's architecture was described as 'monstrous' by garden artist and author Prince Pückler-Muskau, and author Leigh Hunt claimed that Nash was 'a better layer-out of grounds than architect'. Nash's park not only had impressive villas and terraces, but trees, grass and a very attractive artificial lake extending over 22 acres.

Chester Terrace was built in 1825, with three porticoes with projecting Corinthian columns. The magnificent arches at either end were put in by the builder, James Burton, against Nash's wishes. Sculpted figures by J. G. Bubb were taken down at Nash's insistence.

Three societies were present in the park and had a significant impact. The Zoological Society was established in the park in July 1824 at the suggestion of the famous explorer Sir Stamford Raffles. The Commissioners offered the society a 5-acre area on the northeast boundary. Decimus Burton was again commissioned to design many of the society's very elegant buildings, pens, cages and aviaries to house the beasts and birds donated. Members of the public were admitted on weekdays, on payment of a shilling, and the production of a letter of introduction from a Fellow of the society.

Archery has always been an appropriate sport for London's Royal Parks. In 1832 the members of the Toxophilite Society were allotted a 5-acre plot in Regent's Park, with a small rustic lodge erected to serve as a pavilion for the archers. A prominent presence in the park, the society flourished until 1922, when numbers had declined and there were not enough to keep it going.

The Royal Botanical Society of London, founded in the second year of Queen Victoria's reign, rented 18 acres of land in the Inner Circle, and made a significant impact on the landscape of the park. Again Decimus Burton was involved: he was invited to lay out the gardens and design the necessary buildings along with eminent landscape gardener Robert Marnock. For nearly a century, the society's summer flower shows were among the most

Fashion plate showing Sussex Place across the lake in 1838–9.

popular events of the London season. However, by 1932, with rent at unaffordable levels, the society was unable to continue and the Royal Parks Department took over the maintenance of the gardens, by this time renamed in honour of Queen Mary, the wife of King George V.

In January 1861 landscape architect William Andrews Nesfield was called in to advise on much of the planting in the park, which was failing. The designs for the Avenue Gardens, subsequently delivered by his son Markham Nesfield, were impressive and imposing. The gardens included sculpture and tazzas. By January 1863 Nesfield had produced a plan for the flower garden to be laid out in an Italian style and located within the four existing rows of trees.

Elephant rides were popular on the Broad Walk within the park.

The hothouse in the Royal Botanic Gardens held a range of tropical flowers, including the Victoria Regis lily, upon which the secretary of the society could sit in a chair.

By now the park was fully open to the public and attracting the attention of philanthropists, who freely donated sculptures and features to the park — for example the fountain designed by R. Kevile and presented in 1865 by the Indian potentate Sir Cowasji Jehangir Readymoney, which is still in position on the Broad Walk. Sigismund Goetze was another benfactor, who over three decades donated sculptures and fountains of various kinds for the park he so loved, in particular the gilded wrought-iron gates at the entrance to Queen Mary's Gardens.

The twentieth century witnessed the greatest threats to Nash's legacy. The Second World War brought significant damage to the park and the terraces. Several were demolished and a number destroyed, including Holford House. After the war, Nash's vision was threatened with complete demolition and, if the Marylebone Labour Party had had their way, the terraces would have been pulled down and mundane flats built in their place. They were retained as a result of the 1947 Gorell Commission, which recommended full restoration, a conclusion accepted in Cabinet on the casting vote of the Prime Minister, Clement Attlee.

The Royal Botanic Gardens, laid out by Decimus Burton and Robert Marnock, were eventually taken over by the Royal Parks Department and renamed Queen Mary's Gardens.

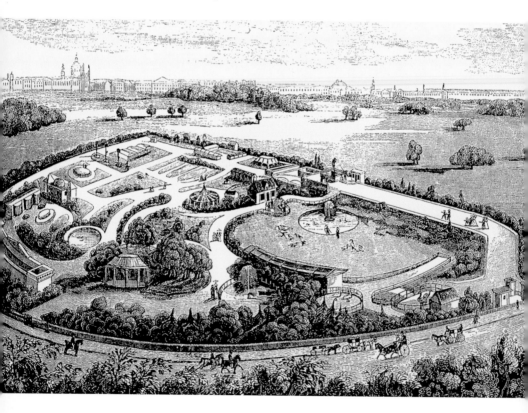

664 REGENTS PARK. — The Fountain. — LL.

The Broad Walk, with the Readymoney Fountain, was the avenue forming the main axis of the park, and was originally intended to lead to the Prince Regent's villa.

The Avenue Gardens and Broad Walk replaced Nash's original avenue of trees between Park Square and Chester Road, which by the 1860s was in poor condition. Nesfield kept two of the four lines of trees, with elms outside horse chestnuts.

In essence, little has changed since that time. The park is a place to return to again and again, whether it is to admire Nash's terraces and villas, to sit in the garden of St John's Lodge, to look upon the splendour of the geraniums in the urns of the Avenue Gardens, or just to wander in and enjoy the 400 acres of open parkland, all thanks to the pertinacity of John Fordyce and the genius of John Nash.

The original bandstand in Regent's Park was near the Readymoney Fountain. A twin of the Kensington Gardens bandstand, this was originally erected in Richmond Park in 1931 but after 1951 fell out of favour and was dismantled and moved to Regent's Park in 1975.

The Jubilee Gates, c. 1935, in Regent's Park were a gift of Sigismund Goetze to commemorate the Silver Jubilee and the official opening of Queen Mary's Gardens in 1935.

GREENWICH PARK: BIRTHPLACE OF THE TUDORS

The Honourable Mrs Evelyn Cecil wrote in 1907:

> ... it would not occur to most people to reckon Greenwich among the London Parks. But it is well within the bounds of the County of London, and now so easy of access that it should have no difficulty in substantiating its claim to be one of the most beautiful among them. Both for natural features and historic interest it is one of the most fascinating.

HISTORICALLY, Greenwich is the oldest of the parklands for, though as a Royal Park it is not as old as St James's Park, it is certainly the oldest of the fenced domains. The land that forms the park was part of Blackheath until Henry VI, in the fifteenth year of his reign, gave his uncle Humphrey, Duke of Gloucester, licence to enclose 200 acres of the wood and heath 'to make a park in Greenwich'. It was a favourite resort long before that: situated on the high ground above the marshy banks of the Thames, Greenwich was found suitable for country residence in Roman times. On one of the hills in the park, with a commanding view over the river, the remains of a Roman villa have been excavated. The Romans were not the first to appreciate this prominent site, however. Twenty-five 'barrows' are present on the southwest corner of the park, near the Crooms Hill Gate, where numerous items have been discovered over many years. There was probably some royal residence at Greenwich from the time of Edward I, but it was not until the arrival of Humphrey, Duke of Gloucester, that the palace much used in Tudor times was built. This building faced the Thames and went by the name of 'Placentia' or 'Plaisance'. The royal licence that gave the Duke leave to enclose a portion of the heath provided that he might also build 'Towers of stone and lime'. A tower stood on the hill now crowned by the Observatory, which was pulled down when Charles II had the Observatory erected from designs by Wren in 1675. During Tudor times, Greenwich was much lived in by the Sovereign, and there were many pageants, jousting, games and May Day frolics. Henry VIII was born here, as was his daughter, Mary Tudor, who was betrothed here to the Dauphin of France.

Flamsteed House in 1835. This original Observatory building was designed by Sir Christopher Wren in 1675 for Charles II. The site also includes the Prime Meridian of the world, the Harrison timekeepers and the UK's largest refracting telescope.

She often resided here during her short and troubled reign. It was also at Greenwich that Queen Elizabeth I was born; and to Greenwich Henry brought his fourth bride, when poor Anne Boleyn's short-lived favour was at an end, and Jane Seymour dead. The less beautiful Anne of Cleves, who so dismally failed to please the King, was escorted in state from Calais by thirty gentlemen, who rode right through the park from the Black Heath to the northern gate and round through the town to the palace, the guns firing from the tower in her honour.

After Elizabeth's accession, 'the City of London entertained the Queen at Greenwich with a muster' on 2 July 1559. 'Goodly banqueting houses' were built of 'fir poles decked with birch branches and all manner of flowers both of the field and garden, as roses, gilly flowers, lavender, marigold, and all manner of strewing herbs and rushes.' Much of this pageantry ended with Elizabeth but the park was much improved by the Stuarts. James I replaced the wooden fence of the park by a brick wall, 12 feet high and 2 miles round. Much of this still remains, although some sections have been replaced by iron railings.

The Queen's House, which is the only portion of the older building that still exists, was begun under James I and completed by Inigo Jones for Queen

During the Second World War, there were anti-aircraft guns in the Flower Garden and the tips of some of the trees were cut off to widen the field of fire. Evidence of this can still be seen in the truncated shapes of some of the trees. After the war, the park was restored to its former glory.

Henrietta Maria, the wife of Charles I. Although the sale does not appear to have been completed, Greenwich was among the Royal Parks that Cromwell's Parliament intended to sell. The deer at the time must have been numerous and in good condition, for during the Commonwealth the fear of their being stolen was such that soldiers were posted in the tower for their preservation.

Charles II, perhaps hating the palace that had been appropriated and lived in by Cromwell, pulled it down and began building a new one and remodelled

View of London from Greenwich Hill, by Johannes Vorsterman (English, seventeenth century).

the park. Le Nôtre's name is associated with the changes at Greenwich, as it was with St James's Park, but it is unlikely that he ever came to England. The alterations were carried out under the superintendence of Sir William Boreman, who became Keeper of the Park. A series of terraces sloping down from the tower formed part of the design, and their outline can still be traced between the Observatory and the Queen's House, which faces the hill at the foot. The old palace had deteriorated considerably, so Charles simply pulled it down and commenced a vast building designed by Wren, only one wing of which was completed in his reign. Charles II, a great supporter of scientific research and instrumental in the foundation of the Royal Society in 1661, commissioned Sir Christopher Wren to build the Royal Observatory, which was then named Flamsteed House after the first Astronomer Royal, John Flamsteed.

The last monarch to use Greenwich was James II; after that royal interest faded. James's daughter Mary donated the palace site as a hospital for sailors and in the early years of the eighteenth century the park was opened to pensioners. During the Georgian era, relatives of the King often held the post of Ranger of Greenwich Park but the park's appearance changed little. In 1873 the Royal Naval Hospital became the Royal Naval College and eventually, in 1933, the Queen's House was restored to create the National Maritime Museum.

During the Second World War anti-aircraft guns were installed in the Flower Garden, and the tops of some of the trees were cut off to provide better lines of fire at enemy bombers that followed the line of the river to seek their targets.

In 1930 a statue of General James Wolfe (1727–59) by Robert Tait Mackenzie was erected above the Great Steps escarpment. Wolfe's parents lived on the edge of Greenwich Park in Macartney House, and the statue commemorates Wolfe's victory over the French at Quebec, although he died in the battle. It was the gift of the Canadian people and was unveiled by the Marquis de Montcalm, a descendant of the defeated French commander-in-chief, who also died in the battle. The statue was damaged by shrapnel in the war. As a result of its World Heritage Site status, the area behind the Wolfe statue was to be reconfigured with more pedestrian space, fewer cars, and inscriptions in the pavement relating to Ptolemy's Planets. Giant steps flanked by pine trees that led down the escarpment from the Wolfe statue no longer exist.

Aptly, the Honourable Lady Evelyn Cecil concludes her description of Greenwich Park in 1907: 'Under the shady trees on a summer's day it would still be

The Lodge, on the Broad Walk in Greenwich Park.

Victorians promenading along the Broad Walk.

possible to dream of Romans and Danes, of pageants and tournaments, and to people the scene with the heroes and heroines of yore' – this is still so relevant today. The buildings in and around Greenwich Park are among the most magnificent in Britain, notable for their historic and scientific connections as well as for their architecture. These have changed little and the view across London is still one of the finest. In 2012 the park was also host to London Olympic events, despite local controversy and concerns about long lasting-damage to the park and the historic landscape.

View to Canary Wharf from Greenwich Park.

BUSHY PARK: A ROYAL SLEEPING BEAUTY

THE LEAST FAMILIAR of all the Royal Parks, Bushy Park comprises areas of deer park, woodland, farmland and water gardens, developed from the late fifteenth century onwards; the park's history is closely connected to the development of Hampton Court Park and its adjacent gardens, from which the park is now separated. The majority of the boundaries of the park are enclosed by walls to this day.

The origins of the deer park at Bushy date from as early as 1491, when Sir Giles Daubeney, Henry VII's Lord Chamberlain, enclosed 300 acres of Middle Park's farmland. By 1504 Cardinal Wolsey, then residing at Hampton Court, had enclosed three areas of farmland, Bushy Park, Middle Park and Hare Warren, and also the Home Park of Hampton Court Palace. Evidence still remains of its former agricultural use, with traces of medieval track, and ditches and field hedges, as well as rabbit warrens. When Henry VIII acquired Hampton Court in 1529 he formed his royal deer park from these enclosed lands, also enclosing Old Park in 1537. Bushy Park was further extended in 1620 when Court Field was enclosed with a wall, the last enclosure of land to form Bushy Park. In 1708 Charles Montagu, Earl of Halifax, a Treasury Lord and later first Chancellor of the Exchequer, purchased the keepership of the three parks from Charles II's former mistress the Duchess of Cleveland. As a result the distinction between Bushy Park, Middle Park and Hare Warren was lost and all became known as Bushy Park.

In 1638–9 Charles I had a tributary of the River Colne diverted through Bushy Park, which was named the Longford River. The new waterway, designed by Nicholas Lane and constructed by Edward Manning, was 12 miles long and entered Bushy Park at Pantile Bridge near Upper Lodge, the oldest of the occupied sites in Bushy Park, in the northwest corner of the park. There were waterworks at various points along the Longford River, including a cascade by Waterhouse Pond dating from 1710. Water from the river was used for the elaborate water gardens created in the grounds of Upper Lodge by the second Earl of Halifax in the eighteenth century. During the Commonwealth, water had been diverted to feed the new Heron and Leg of Mutton Ponds.

Opposite: The restored Diana Fountain in 2013.

Queen Adelaide's
Lodge (Bushy
House), in an
engraving by
Thomas Allom
(1804–72).

The Lower Lodge was built by the Keeper of Middle Park in 1663–5. It later became the residence of the Ranger of Bushy Park, a post held by members of the aristocracy and the Royal Family until 1896, and eventually it became known as Bushy House. Among those to have served as Ranger was King William IV while Duke of Clarence (1797–1830). To ensure that his wife and consort, Queen Adelaide, could remain at their long-time home after his death, he appointed her as his successor as Ranger and she held the post until her death in 1849.

The main avenues of Bushy Park were first planted in 1689–99 under the direction of the Royal Gardener, George London, with Henry Wise contracted in 1699. The park was – and still is – essentially divided by the impressive Chestnut Avenue, with its chestnuts and outer rows of limes, which extends north from the Lion Gates of Hampton Court Palace as far as Teddington Lodge. It is interrupted just to the north by the misnamed 'Diana Fountain', a circular basin which was made in 1699 with a central pedestal; in 1713 a statue actually representing Arethusa with attendant figures was erected here; it had previously been located in the Privy Garden at Hampton Court. Impressive lime avenues extend west from the Diana Fountain for nearly a mile, and there are numerous other extensive avenues, also mainly lime.

The Upper Lodge and its 15 acres of gardens designed for the Earl of Halifax received wide acclaim in the eighteenth century. These elaborate water gardens, formed from the Longford River, had pools and a cascade enhanced by rustic stone grottoes and grassy paths, offset with clipped yew, holly and box. The present house was built on the site of the previous Ranger's Lodge, which was in ruins by 1710, when the Earl of Halifax became Ranger of Bushy Park; it was a condition of his tenancy that he rebuilt the house. The original Georgian design of his house has been overlaid by additions and extensions, particularly in the nineteenth century, when, following the establishment of the Office of Works, Upper Lodge became one of the 'grace and favour' residences at the disposal of the sovereign. The last grace and favour tenant, the widow of General Lord Alfred Paget, left in 1913 and George V allowed it to be used by the Canadian Red Cross during the First World War. It became known as the King's Canadian Hospital; a prefabricated theatre built to entertain the convalescing Canadian soldiers still stands. In 1919 it was granted to the London County Council as a holiday home for underprivileged boys from the East End of London, known as the 'King's Canadian School'. It accommodated 290 boys, who frequently used the pools for swimming after their open-air lessons.

Attributed to a master of seventeenth-century bronzes, Hubert Le Sueur, the Diana Fountain was originally called 'Arethusa', after the nymph in Ovid's *Metamorphoses* who was rescued by Diana. Charles I had the fountain designed for his queen, Henrietta Maria. Drawing by H. B. Ziegler; engraving by E. Duncan.

Bushy House in
an 1827 book
illustration.

In 1901 work
began on
converting the
ground floor
and basement of
Bushy House
into a physics
laboratory. Other
parts of the
building were
arranged as
temporary
laboratories for
electrical, magnetic
and thermometric
work, in addition
to metallurgical
and chemical
research.

At the start of the Second World War the site was requisitioned by the
Air Ministry and in June 1942 the US 8th Army Air Force set up camp in
Bushy Park, with Upper Lodge designated as a barracks for enlisted men.
After the war, in 1945 Upper Lodge was transferred to the Admiralty and

'The review in Bushy Park – Charge of the 10th Hussars' (1871).

used as an extension of the Admiralty Research Station based at the National Physical Laboratory. During the twentieth century various 'temporary' buildings were erected. The requisition was converted to a formal lease and the next few decades saw a determined struggle between the Ministry of Works, which was responsible for management of Royal Parks, and the Admiralty, which wanted to erect more buildings on the grounds.

To a large extent the park is the creation of William, Duke of Clarence, and in essence has changed little since 1850. It was while he was Ranger there that most of the stands of oaks, which now form such a prominent feature of the park, were planted. After William became king and lost interest in farming Bushy, large areas he had enclosed for agriculture were returned to parkland. The farm buildings were demolished and the Stockyard, with its barns, stables and venison house is now used as the administrative centre for the park.

There was little further change through the nineteenth century, despite the park becoming more accessible to the public. During her reign, Queen Victoria opened Bushy Park to the public and they flocked to enjoy this beautiful open space. Particularly popular were the displays of chestnut blossoms in late spring and the tradition of parading down Chestnut Avenue on the Sunday closest to 11 May (the date on which the blossoms are reputed to be at their finest). Even members of the Royal Family were known to take part in Chestnut Sunday. Suspended during the First World War, it was resurrected in peacetime. Bus companies ran special excursions from London. During the First World War, some areas were again put under the plough as temporary allotments, which remained in place for many years

afterwards. Chestnut Sunday was gradually losing its popularity with the servant class, to whom a Sunday off was a rare treat. It was eventually abandoned, but was resurrected for Queen Elizabeth II's Silver Jubilee in 1977, and continues to this day.

The Boating Pool, the triangular pool at the end of the Heron Pond, is a result of a government scheme after the end of the First World War to provide work for the unemployed in the Royal Parks. It was incredibly popular, with small rowboats and pedalos for hire. These lasted until the 1970s, when their popularity declined and the pool simply became too expensive to maintain. A similar scheme was created by Mr Hepburn, Park Superintendent, using the unemployed to help create a new garden in Waterhouse Wood. The workforce cleared undergrowth and Hepburn created a woodland dell with a profusion of exotic plants and flowers such as azaleas. Cascades were made from a tributary of the Longford River and rustic bridges and winding paths completed the transformation into one of the then fashionable 'paradise gardens'. Later Superintendents, such as J. M. Fisher (who was responsible for the Isabella Plantation in Richmond Park), carried out further improvements, opening up land beneath trees as informal lawns and adding the impressive swamp cypresses which gave local children their own 'Fairyland', as it was popularly known.

The Second World War saw areas returned to growing food, and temporary buildings were erected to replace bombed-out London offices; these were collectively known as Camp Griffiss. Large numbers of troops were billeted here and the camp even included a cinema, sports pitches and a landing strip. As well as the camp, the Diana Fountain and the ponds were shrouded in camouflage netting. At its peak nearly eight thousand troops were stationed in Bushy Park. In 1944 General Eisenhower took over part of

Camp Griffiss during the Second World War, now commemorated by a plaque in the park.

Camp Griffiss as the Supreme Headquarters of the Allied Expeditionary Force. It was here that the Normandy invasion was planned, and the chestnut blossoms that year bore silent witness to the agonising decisions that faced the Allied Forces in the last weeks of the planning process. The American camp survived until the early 1960s, when it was bulldozed. A memorial now exists on the site with a dedication from the Royal Air Force to their American comrades-in-arms.

Bushy Park is now very much a gentle landscape, a 'royal Sleeping Beauty', despite being ravaged in the great hurricane of 1987 when hundreds of magnificent oaks and limes were destroyed overnight. The Upper Lodge

The USAF base at Camp Griffiss, in Bushy Park.

A View of the Cascade, Bushy Park Water Garden, c. 1715 (oil on canvas), from the studio of Marco Ricci (1676–1730). The restored gardens bear a very close resemblance to this painting.

Water Gardens restoration plans got under way in the 1990s, with research and a report instigated and undertaken by the Friends of Bushy and Home Parks (helped by the discovery by Sir Roy Strong of an eighteenth-century painting of the gardens). The Royal Parks built on this early work and secured Heritage Lottery Fund funding and management responsibility

Summer dining in Bushy Park Woodland Garden.

for the site in 2006, allowing restoration work to begin. The restoration included de-silting and returning the ponds to their original shape and depth, and overhauling the water engineering system to restore the direct connection to the Longford River. The badly damaged southern flank cascade wall was carefully reconstructed, reincorporating original stonework and bricks into the new structure, and the cascade and northern flank wall were also restored.

The Bushy Park of today has a timeless, secret atmosphere. The political grandees, the royals, the Tudor schemers with their enclosures, the medieval tenant farmers and the first users of the land over four thousand years ago have all left their imprint on the grasslands of Bushy Park.

Restored lime avenues in Bushy Park, which were devastated during the storm of 1987.

87

RICHMOND PARK: A MEDIEVAL ROYAL PASTURE

THERE MAY HAVE BEEN a manor house at Richmond-upon-Thames as early as 1066, though the name Richmond would not be associated with the place until four centuries later. When first recorded, it belonged to King Henry I (1100–35) and would have been a typical country house of the period; the manor was called 'Shene'. By the fourteenth century, Shene was a particularly important royal house, with King Richard II's first wife Anne especially fond of the place. But with the plague raging in London in 1394, many moved out to Shene and sadly Queen Anne caught an infection and died within hours. Overcome by grief, Richard ordered the manor to be razed to the ground.

It was Henry VII who built up Shene again on a much grander scale but in 1499 the riverside buildings were burnt to the ground with great losses. Henry rebuilt on an even grander scale and it became Richmond Palace because the king also happened to be the Earl of Richmond in North Yorkshire.

The name 'Shene' was kept for the east and west parts of the ancient manorial lands. During the early part of his reign, Henry VIII was also very fond of Richmond but soon lost interest when he saw the even grander palace that Cardinal Wolsey was raising for himself upstream at Hampton Court. It was Wolsey who offered Hampton Court to Henry and, in return, he was invited by the king to use the palace at Richmond. Wolsey was not resident for long and eventually took refuge in a lodge that was part of the old monastery of Shene. When Henry took over the monastery lands he turned them into a royal game preserve, now known as the Old Deer Park.

It was, however, the 'New Park' at Richmond that became Richmond Park; it was the personal creation of Charles I, who wanted a new hunting ground away from the City of London, where Hyde Park was no longer as private as he wished. He decided to enclose 2,500 acres of unspoiled land and create a much better hunting reserve, against significant local opposition – his idea did not appeal to most of the local landowners, whose property he needed. There was also influential political opposition, including the King's Exchequer, which recognised the enormous cost of purchasing so much land

Opposite: Richmond Palace from the southwest, c. 1630. Detail from a painting (artist unknown) in the Fitzwilliam Museum.

The Carlile Family with Sir Justinian Isham in Richmond Park by Joan Carlile (1600–79).

and of enclosing the park with such a long stretch of brick wall (almost 10 miles). However, many of the landowners gradually gave in, knowing that their best option was to obtain any adequate compensation.

The end of the Civil War saw great changes to Richmond. The royal palace at the foot of the hill was sold by Parliamentarians and started to deteriorate until it was almost beyond repair. The New Park at Richmond was chiefly valued at this time as a prime source of venison and was given to the City of London; as a consequence, deer stocks suffered, although the park's infrastructure was well maintained. With the return of King Charles II from exile, he offered Richmond Palace to his mother, the dowager queen, Henrietta Maria, who preferred the Queen's House at Greenwich. Sadly, as a result, Richmond Palace was pulled down but the park was returned to Crown ownership and for a century and a half was enjoyed by most members of successive royal families.

On the death of his father, George I, in 1727, George II appointed Sir Robert Walpole to the post of Ranger of Richmond Park. Sir Robert held this very responsible post for several years, and his impact on the park was significant. At once he set about draining the park: it had been boggy, overgrown and a haunt of poachers and Walpole and his co-Ranger converted it into a well-stocked hunting ground including over three thousand wild turkeys. It became popular with the monarch, who required a 'shooting box' in this quiet rural retreat. Constructed with Portland stone, the New Lodge was regularly used during the summer months by the King and Queen. Walpole had already spent a significant amount of his own money improving the Old Lodge for his own use and enjoyment and would spend most of his weekends there, insisting he could work better in the countryside than he could in the rage and bustle of the town.

Walpole had strong views on public access to Richmond Park and felt that the amount of money he had spent on improvements to the park entitled him to privacy and freedom from casual intruders in his leisure moments. It was Walpole who had the old 'ladder-stile' gates removed from the walls of the park, for by these the enclosed land could be entered freely at almost any point on the park's perimeter. He had small lodges built beside the official park gates and installed strong and capable keepers, who were given strict instructions that they should admit only 'respectable persons' in the daytime, again much to the strong protestations of local people.

Keeper's House in Richmond Park, 1757, by Joshua Gosselin (1739–1813).

A Lodge in Richmond Park, the residence of Philip Medows Esq, 1780. Engraved by W. Watts from a drawing by G. Barret.

The troubles became especially serious in 1751 when the Princess Amelia, the King's youngest daughter, took over the Rangership of the park. She moved into the Old Lodge, treating the park as if it was her own private property, and closed it to the public altogether, admitting her own personal friends, but granting only very few special permits. Again, local inhabitants were infuriated but the Princess stood firm. For several years there were legal skirmishes, with one notable case brought by a brewer called John Lewis, who was determined to carry on the struggle for open access; his persistence resulted in a court appearance at Kingston Assizes on 3 April 1758. Lewis based his case on the rights of way granted by King Charles I to those on foot. The verdict given was in Lewis's favour. Within a month of the assizes at Kingston, ladder-stiles fitted with gates had been built like bridges over the park walls near East Sheen and Ham. The devious Princess Amelia was infuriated by the decision and ordered that the rungs on the ladder-stiles should be spaced so far apart that only the most athletic could hope to use them. Lewis once again appealed to the law and the learned judge, Mr Justice Foster, was entirely sympathetic: 'And I desire, Mr Lewis, that you would see it so constructed that not only children and old men, but old women, too, may be able to get up.'

Lewis became a local popular hero, and Princess Amelia, who had become even more unpopular, gave up the Rangership of the park to George III shortly after his accession.

In Princess Amelia's place George III appointed John Stuart, the Third Earl of Bute, who went to live in the New Lodge. Both George III and John Stuart took a lively interest in the upkeep of the park and many improvements were made: local people were given better access and relations with them were repaired. With the death of the Earl of Bute, King George III took back the Rangership into his own keeping and with real enthusiasm announced that he intended to have all the swampy parts of the park drained, 'the roads turned where beauty and advantage could be gained by so doing', and the open parts ornamented with plantations. Sadly, wars with France and a mysterious illness curtailed such enthusiasm. The New Lodge, by now known as the White Lodge, was occupied by Viscount Sidmouth, better known as Henry Addington. In 1813 Sidmouth was made Deputy Ranger of the park, and a year later the Princess Elizabeth, daughter of King George III, was given the Rangership.

Large areas of the park, which already contained some older timber, were enclosed and the plantations that are so prominent today were established, including Spankers Hill, planted in 1819 with oak, larch, spruce, sweet chestnut and other trees, and the Sidmouth Plantation in 1823, planted mainly with sweet chestnuts, a smaller number of oaks, and a few fine beeches.

The eastern side of the Upper and Lower Pen Ponds, created after Charles I's enclosure of this area, was planted to form the Pond Plantation in 1824, again mainly with oaks, with the western and southern areas being planted later in the century. In 1825 the Hamcross Plantation was added to

Between the
Pen Ponds.

	MILES	YARDS
RICHMOND GATE	-1-	1140
ROEHAMPTON GATE-	-	1450
ROBIN HOOD GATE	-2-	190
" " BY ROEHAMPTON " "	-1-	1490
" " BY WHITE LODGE		
KINGSTON GATE	-3-	200
HAM GATE - - - -	-2-	760

Distance plate in Richmond Park, which allowed the gatekeepers to inform park users of the distance to the next gate – a frequently asked question.

the Park. The Conduit Plantation, consisting almost entirely of oaks, was brought into being in 1829, given its name because it stands on the site of one of the three conduits that supplied water to King Henry VII's palace at Richmond.

In 1831 work started on what was to become known as Isabella Plantation, and while such improvements were being carried out the keepers at the entrance lodges were said to be 'remarkable for their civility' and freely admitted carriages whose owners had obtained orders from Lord Sidmouth, together with virtually all comers on foot.

With such vast numbers visiting the park, there were those who were less welcome – including large groups who came for the purpose of hunting squirrels. In 1834, nearby Petersham Park was bought for £14,500 and absorbed into the larger expanse of Richmond Park with the creation of the Terrace Walk between Richmond Gate and the stables of Pembroke Lodge.

Near the Terrace Walk, at the north end of the Pembroke Lodge gardens, there is a hillock known as King Henry the Eighth's Mound, thought by many originally to have been a barrow; subsequent generations have been told that this was the spot on which Henry VIII stood, on 19 May 1536, while he was watching for a rocket that would be fired, in or near the Tower of London, to tell him that his unfaithful wife Anne Boleyn had duly been executed, and that he was legally and morally free to marry her successor, Lady Jane Seymour. However, this is more than likely simple folklore and legend, rather than reality.

RICHMOND PARK THE ENTRANCE.

Richmond Gate is one of the original six gates and has the heaviest traffic. The gates were widened in 1896.

Richmond Park, near the Kingston Gate.

After Lord Sidmouth's death in 1844, the White Lodge again became a royal home, with the Duchess of Gloucester (Queen Victoria's aunt) living there. In 1858, Albert, Prince of Wales, was installed in the Lodge but three years later Queen Victoria herself moved into the place after her mother had

The White Lodge in 2013, now a ballet school.

RICHMOND PARK

Richmond Park is a leading site for ancient trees, particularly oaks, which have great historic and ecological importance. There are about 1,200 ancient trees, some of which pre-date the park's enclosure.

died. The Old Lodge, Walpole's principal country retreat, was found to be in a poor state in 1838 and was demolished in 1841. Other buildings in the park remained, including The Thatched House Lodge, Sheen Cottage and Pembroke Lodge (the boyhood home of philosopher Bertrand Russell). But Richmond Park is not about buildings, monuments or public art. It is unique among the Royal Parks of London, with its 2,500 acres, and only 6 miles from the centre of London. Successive Rangers, Keepers and Superintendents have managed to preserve this lusty, spacious and almost untamed landscape. Despite the profusion of cars and the hordes of visitors, including a constant parade of cyclists, and the roar of noisy aircraft as they pass overhead, it is refreshingly simple to lose oneself in this rustic yet enchanting landscape. The trees that adorn this landscape are largely indigenous, dating back to Lord Sidmouth and his associates who started their plantations just after the Napoleonic Wars, and there are 70,000 of them, all English hardwoods such as beech, chestnut, hawthorn, hornbeam, oak and rowan, and planted in less than two decades after Mr G.J. Brown, Chief Forester on the Harewood Estate in Yorkshire, became Superintendent of Richmond Park in 1951. There are no exotics here! Among these majestic trees, deer roam freely, nearly three hundred red deer and a similar number of fallow deer, and they have done since 1529. The deer today are managed to keep the stock in the finest possible condition. A certain proportion of the resulting venison is allocated to the royal table, to certain officers of the crown, and to others entitled by royal warrant to a haunch for their own use, including the Prime Minister, members of the Cabinet and a number of Archbishops.

Today, the park is a haven for wildlife. Its designation as a Site of Special Scientific Interest in 1992 and its status as a National Nature Reserve are no accident. These designations are on account of the assemblage of veteran trees and the saproxylic invertebrates – particularly stag beetles – that are associated with them, along with the largest area of lowland acid grassland in the Greater London area. The Pen Ponds are well stocked with fish of various kinds and the park's birdlife is rich. There may not now be as many occasional visitors of great rarity as there were when C. L. Collenette completed, in the mid 1930s, his classic study of the birds in Richmond Park, but the variety of birdlife more than satisfies local and visiting birdwatchers.

Other recent changes that have impacted on the park include the erection of the Roehampton Housing Estate, which looks down on the park at its northeast corner, and the opening of the Isabella Plantation to the public and

The view from the top of Richmond Park westward to Windsor has inspired artists such as J. M. W. Turner and writers; one particularly grand description of the view can be found in Sir Walter Scott's novel *The Heart of Midlothian* (1818). The view from Pembroke Lodge is enjoyed by many of the diners at and visitors to this restored building in the park.

Herds of red and fallow deer roam freely within much of the park. A cull takes place each November and February to ensure that their numbers remain sustainable.

Isabella Plantation in spring – now carefully managed by the Royal Parks to maintain a balance between public access and biodiversity.

its subsequent and ongoing development. It was once an impenetrable and overgrown thicket, but a small stream now flows through it, and glades have been cleared and planted with a myriad of azaleas. Heathers, primulas and many other flowering plants make a spectacular display in spring and early summer. It is very different from the subdued surrounding landscape of Richmond Park.

Richmond Park was described in 1956 by Richard Church as:

> ... a great repository of history, and especially Royal history, the tale of our kings and queens, and the part they have played in the growth of our democratic way of life, a way which works because of the things shared between all the people; the rights, privileges, and constitutional pleasures, such as these Royal Parks so substantially represent... but having in common that Englishness which is so difficult to define, but which we recognise instantly, when we enter the gates of Richmond Park at any point.

One of the many veteran oak trees that remain in the park.

RICHMOND
PARK

Chorley & Pickersgill Ltd Lithographers Leeds

FURTHER READING

Baxter Brown, Michael. *Richmond Park: The History of a Royal Deer Park.*
   Robert Hale Ltd, 1985.

Cecil, The Hon. Mrs Evelyn. *London Parks and Gardens.* Archibald Constable
   & Co. Ltd, 1907.

Cloake, John. *Richmond Palace: Its History and Its Plan.* Richmond Local
   History Society, 2000.

Collenette, C. L. *A History of Richmond Park.* Sidgwick & Jackson Ltd, 1937.
   Dancy, Eric. *Hyde Park.* Methuen & Co. Ltd, 1937.

Green, David. *The Gardens and Parks at Hampton Court and Bushy.*
   Department of Environment, HMSO, 1974.

Gusov, Sasha. *The Royal Parks of London: A Journey through the Parks.*
   Hurtwood Press, 2011.

Karter, John. *Guide to Richmond Park.* The Friends of Richmond Park, 2011.

Lasdun, Susan. *The English Park: Royal, Private and Public.*
   Andre Deutsch, 1991.

McDowall, David. *Richmond Park: The Walker's Historical Guide.*
   David McDowall, 1996.

Rabbitts, Paul. *Regent's Park, From Tudor Hunting Ground to the Present.*
   Amberley, 2013.

Rabbitts, Paul. *Richmond Park: from Medieval Pasture to Royal Park.*
   Amberley, 2014.

Summerson, John. *John Nash, Architect to King George IV.* George Allen
   & Unwin, 1934.

Trench, Lucy. *Buildings and Monuments in the Royal Parks.*
   The Royal Parks, 1997.

Tweedie, Mrs Alec. *Hyde Park: Its History and Romance.*
   Besant & Co. Ltd, 1930.

Webster, A. D. *Greenwich Park: Its History and Associations.*
   Harper Collins, 1971.

White, Kathy, and Foster, Peter. *Bushy Park: Royals, Rangers and Rogues.*
   Foundry Press, 1997.

Opposite:
Richmond Park, by
Emilio Camilio
Leopoldo Tafani
(1920), one of
the destinations
advertised by
Underground
Electric Railways
Company Ltd.

PLACES TO VISIT

Apsley House (English Heritage), 149 Piccadilly, Hyde Park Corner, London W1J 7NT.
   Telephone: 0870 333 1181. Website: www.english-heritage.co.uk

Historic Royal Palaces. Telephone: 0844 482777. Website: www.hrp.org.uk
   The Banqueting House, Whitehall, London SW1A 2ER.
   Hampton Court Palace, Surrey KT8 9AU.
   Kensington Palace, Kensington Gardens, London W8 4PX.
   Kew Palace, Royal Botanic Gardens, Richmond, Surrey TW9 3AB.

The Household Cavalry Museum, Horse Guards, Whitehall SW1A 2AX. Telephone: 020 7930 3070.
   Website: www.householdcavalrymuseum.co.uk

Marlborough House, Pall Mall, London SW1Y 5HX. Website: www.ucl.ac.uk

Old Richmond Palace, Richmond Council, Richmond Green, The Green Richmond, Surrey
   TW9 1LX. Telephone: 08456 122660. Website: www.visitrichmond.co.uk

Palace of Westminster, Westminster, London SW1A 0AA.
   Website: www.parliament.uk/visiting/visiting-and-tours

Royal Botanic Gardens, Kew, Richmond, Surrey TW9 3AB. Telephone: 020 8332 5655.
   Website: www.kew.org

Royal Collection Trust. Telephone: 020 7766 7300. Website: www.royalcollection.org.uk
   The State Rooms, Buckingham Palace, London SW1A 1AA.
   Clarence House, Little St James's Street, London SW1A 1BA.
   The Royal Mews, Buckingham Palace, London SW1W 1QH.

Royal Museums Greenwich. Telephone: 020 8858 4422. Website: ww.rmg.co.uk
   National Maritime Museum, Romney Road, Greenwich, SE10 9NF.
   Cutty Sark, King William Walk, Greenwich SE10 9HT.
   The Queens House, Greenwich, London SE10 9NF.
   Royal Observatory Greenwich, Blackheath Avenue, Greenwich SE10 8XJ.

The Royal Parks, The Old Police House, Hyde Park, London W2 2UH. Telephone: 020 7298 2005.
   Website: www.royalparks.org.uk

Serpentine Gallery, Koenig Books, Kensington Gardens, London W2 3XA. Telephone: 020 7402
   6075. www.serpentinegalleries.org

Wellington Arch (English Heritage), Apsley Way, Hyde Park Corner, London W1J 7JZ.
   Telephone: 0870 333 1181. Website:www.english-heritage.co.uk

Westminster Abbey, 20 Deans Yard, London SW1P 3PA. Telephone: 0207222 5152.
   Website www.westminster-abbey.org

ZSL London Zoo, Regent's Park, London NW1 4RY. Telephone: 020 7722 3333.
   Website: www.zsl.org

INDEX